WHILE CREATION WAITS . . .

WHILE CREATION WAITS

A Christian Response to the Environmental Challenge

Dale & Sandy Larsen

Harold Shaw Publishers
Wheaton, Illinois

Copyright © 1992 by Dale and Sandy Larsen

ISBN 0-87788-949-X

Cover photo © 1992 by Dietrich Photography

Library of Congress Cataloging-in-Publication Data

Larsen, Dale.
   While creation waits : a Christian response to the environmental challenge / Dale Larsen & Sandy Larsen.
      p. cm.
   Includes bibliographical references.
   ISBN 0-87788-949-X
   1. Human ecology—Religious aspects—Christianity. 2. Nature—Religious aspects—Christianity. I. Larsen, Sandy. II. Title.
BT695.5.L37 1992
261.8'362—dc20   92-4944
                                              CIP

99 98 97 96 95 94 93 92

10 9 8 7 6 5 4 3 2 1

The authors owe a great debt of gratitude to the staff of the Au Sable Institute of Environmental Studies (Mancelona, Michigan). In their help and interest in this project they were both professionally knowledgeable and warmly personal.

Our thanks also to Mark Peterson, then Director of the Sigurd Olson Environmental Institute (Ashland, Wisconsin), who originally encouraged us to pursue the writing of a book on a Christian view of ecology.

Contents

PART ONE
DISTORTED VISION

CHAPTER ONE
THE GOOD LIFE?

"What do you expect? Think we were sent into the world
to have a soft time and—what is it?—'float on flowery beds of ease'?
Think Man was just made to be happy?"
*Sinclair Lewis, **Babbitt***

At the top edge of Wisconsin, the Bayfield Peninsula juts northeast into Lake Superior. Forests of spruce and aspen ride the rocky hills; in the interior, sand barrens grow jackpine, blueberries, and black bears. It's a remote place, a place where nature knocks at your door year-round. Apple orchards, an Ojibwe Indian reservation, logging operations, and several small towns share the seclusion of the peninsula.

Offshore are the wooded Apostle Islands with their five historic lighthouses. Only one of the islands is inhabited by humans. The islands attract wealthy boaters in summer, and the October "Apple Fest" pulls in thousands of tourists. Most of the year, however, the peninsula is sparsely populated. Winter weekdays you can ski the National Forest trails and scarcely meet another person.

One narrow highway skirts the peninsula's edge; one blacktop road, County "C," crosses it. All throughout is a maze of logging roads and snowmobile trails where the best of maps is confusing.

Who Lives Here?

Down the dirt roads—no power lines in sight—here and there in the least expected spot, stands a surprising mailbox where a freshly rutted lane disappears into the trees.

Who lives back there? Not the fainthearted. Not people who love crowds and crave the bright lights of the city. The peninsula attracts independent types. And it holds onto people who grew up here and fear the outside world.

Recently an oil company was eager to drill test sites in the Bayfield area. Some of the locals liked the idea of the possible cash that oil would bring to a struggling seasonal economy.

Others were appalled—like the young mother who spoke up at a meeting of an environmental group. "We moved here to get *away* from development," she said. "Now it's coming after us. We have the healthy environment here that we want. How can we keep it from being spoiled?"

The young woman wants to preserve her chosen way of life. She's not really so different from John Falen, a Nevada rancher whose four thousand beef cattle graze on public land that he leases from the Bureau of Land Management.

No moo in '92
Herding beef cattle is a chancy life, with all the risks of weather and markets, but until May 1991 John Falen was "a broad-shouldered study in job satisfaction." Then environmentalism began to encroach on the cattleman's range. The BLM barred him from summer pastures he has leased since 1977, because his thirsty cattle trample the banks of creeks that are home to an endangered species of trout (Turque, "The War for the West," *Newsweek*).

CATTLE FREE BY '93 and NO MOO IN '92 read bumper stickers in the West, and it's not only trout the ecological activists are

4

worried about. The Audubon Society claims that cattle-grazing on the Western plains has led to "a near ecological collapse on public grasslands of the West" (Daggett, "Western Range Reels Under Cattle Onslaught," *Audubon Activist*).

While Audubon fights for higher grazing fees, Falen the rancher is furious at the BLM's environmental restrictions. He says, "I never figured I'd be fighting my own government to defend my way of life."

A day in Earth Court

The cattle rancher and the young mother have strong personal visions of an ideal life, and they will defend them passionately. They aren't alone. In November 1990, a mock "Earth Court" was held on the steps of the Wisconsin State Capitol to "try" Governor Tommy Thompson for his support of new mining in the north. He was charged with (among other things) "callous disregard for the biotic and social communities of Northern Wisconsin." Witnesses—actors in costume—included a bear, a tree, a fish, and a river (Rabe, "A Day in Earth Court," *GreenNet*).

The Madison mock court was sponsored in part by the Greens, a loosely-organized movement for simpler living and decentralization of political and economic power. You do not have to be around a "Green" very long to realize that earthier living is, for them, no sacrifice. They like the local-powered, low-tech life and feel this is the way everyone should live.

In a voice less strident than the Earth Court, a list distributed at a Greens meeting suggests "101 Things You Can Do to Promote Green Values." Some of their lower-key suggestions:

- Mend and repair, rather than discard and replace.
- Eat foods low on the food chain, not meat.
- Turn off lights when not in use.

Just scraping by at $60,000

One family in San Antonio is doing all of the above—and not liking it one bit. They make $60,000 a year and feel like they're "just scraping by." They say, "We just keep repairing old cars. We've cut out all red meat. We try to eat more vegetables and we try to use as little electricity as possible. We feel like we're almost at our limit" (Levinson, "Living on the Edge," *Newsweek).*

To that San Antonio family, the vision of a "Green" world is a recipe for hardship. They're putting up with the simpler life for now, but you get the distinct feeling that as soon as they get more money, they'll junk their old car, buy a new one, and go out for a steak dinner—leaving all the lights on at home.

The cattle rancher, the young mother, the trial witnesses, and the San Antonio family would never agree on how to vote on any environmental issue. What's fascinating, however, is that on a deeper level *they all come remarkably close to saying the same thing.* Their methods are different, but their aim is the same: *to protect what they consider is the Good Life.*

More in Common than They Know

As we've worked on this book, the piles of environmental material have grown ever higher on our desk, now and then cascading onto the floor and into the wastebasket. It's diverse stuff. There are arguments for zero population growth and arguments for unlimited economic expansion. There are scholarly articles both proving and discrediting global warming. There are statistics that our forests are being depleted and equally convincing evidence that our forests are being replenished.

But the more you read the literature on all sides of the ecological crisis, the closer the combatants sound in one basic fear, one assumption, and one egoism.

First, the fear. The people we've met in this chapter so far, and those we've met in our cascading stacks, are all *afraid that their preferred way of life—their hard-won and closely guarded ideal of how things should be—is going to be lost.*

Beneath that fear is a basic shared assumption: No matter which side they're on, they assume that their favorite lifestyle is the one that ought to be protected. They hold the same truth to be self-evident: *that their vision of the Good Life is the right one.*

And beneath the assumption is a common egoism: Whether Green or industrialist, cattle rancher or Audubon member, oil well driller or woods dweller, they all assume that *they're the ones to define nature and decide what's to be done with it.*

A universal attitude

Perhaps this is why books on ecology—from all sides—tend to induce guilt within the first three pages. They present the way things ought to be, and if you don't agree with the writers' visions of utopia, you're an enemy of the good, or at best unenlightened and in need of rehabilitation.

We believe the ecological crisis springs directly from this human arrogance—the certainty that *we,* apart from God, can decide and declare how nature ought to be used. Because this arrogance is inherently human, it occurs on all sides of the debate. The same arrogance that causes the exploitation of nature thus infects the discussion of what to do to heal nature.

That's not to say that all lifestyles are equally good for the earth. There are obviously ways of living that are more in harmony with nature and more respectful of life than other ways. But if we analyze them, we find that the arguments of even the most ecologically conscious are usually based not on what's best for the earth, but on preserving—even enforcing—a particular vision of a preferred way of life.

The irony is that while many of us are jealously protecting our way of life, we are chronically dissatisfied with the very lifestyle we're protecting.

Mutual jealousy

"Class of '73" was so distraught that he resorted to writing to Ann Landers. He felt inadequate, he said, when he compared himself with his college classmates. He wasn't as successful; he hadn't made it like they had.

After the "Class of '73" letter was printed, a woman wrote in to tell the other side of the story:

My husband is probably one of the guys he admires. We have moved six times in 10 years, always for a better paying, more prestigious job. Each move requires establishing new friendships and becoming part of the community. I dream of staying in one place long enough for my children to develop ongoing relationships, but I know it will never happen.

We drive the BMW that "Class of '73" admires as a status symbol. Actually, we have two. Sounds wonderful? Not really. What I wouldn't give for a husband who is satisfied with his job, his salary and the city we live in. My husband's lucky that I am committed to keeping our family life strong and loving. Some days I feel like throwing in the towel. I envy your wife, Mr. "Class of '73." (Ashland, Wisconsin *Daily Press,* Sept. 26, 1991)

If material abundance and convenience equal personal happiness, we should be the happiest people who ever lived. If labor-saving technology equals more time to spare, we should have the most free time of any society since the end of slavery. But where is the evidence that we are happy and free?

In a recent poll of 500 adults, 69 percent said they would like to "slow down and live a more relaxed life," in contrast to 19 percent who said they would like to "live a more exciting, faster-paced life." And 61 percent of those polled agreed with the depressing statement that "earning a living today requires so much effort that it's difficult to find time to enjoy life" (Castro, "The Simple Life," *Time*).

A couple of weeks ago we and a few other people helped some friends move. In appreciation they've invited all of us to come for dessert. There was only one date available when we could all make it between the middle of October and the end of the year, and one of us will have to be late for that because of a prior commitment. We're running into the same time snag with a "round robin" social group of eight people organized by our church. And this, you must remember, is here on the remote shores of Lake Superior, where visitors ask, "What do you *do* here?"

A Promise Unfulfilled

Certainly we would be happy and never want for anything again if advertising lived up to its own promises. But it doesn't dare. Our economy is dependent on promising satisfaction through the purchase of goods and services, but it is even more dependent on keeping us dissatisfied so we continue to purchase more. Therefore our economy, which operates on the promise of material satisfaction, would collapse if everyone achieved satisfaction. In order to function, it must withhold the very satisfaction it promises.

While doing research at the Au Sable Institute of Environmental Studies, a Christian environmental center, we were shown a "contentment graph" that demonstrates how well-being increases with increased possessions—to a point. Then well-being goes down as possessions go up.

CONTENTMENT GRAPH

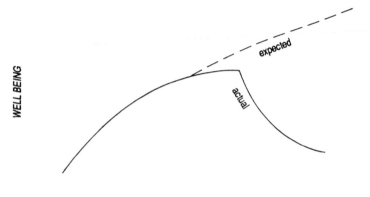

Of course the mainstream of American culture does not believe these statistics and maintains stubborn faith in happiness through progress. We go out to make the world as we think the world should be, and we believe that every day in every way things are getting better and better. When they aren't, we sue.

Life does not always go as we want, of course, and the result is an ingrained grumpiness in the midst of all our prosperity, an ache that we expect somebody else to soothe. Our congenital discontent is transforming the American character into what *Time* magazine called a nation of "crybabies" (demanding rights without responsibilities) and "busybodies" (enforcing regimentation in the name of tolerance).

As one writer put it:

Most religions preach a philosophical endurance of the imperfections of the world. Suffering must be borne. Americans did not come to the New World to live like that. They operate on a pushy, querulous assumption of perfectibility on earth ("the pursuit of happiness"—their own personal happiness). (Morrow, "A Nation of Finger Pointers," *Time*)

"Unrealistic expectations of the modern, risk-avoiding age": that's where our chronic blaming of others comes from, according to William Gaston, public affairs professor at the University of Maryland. We have infinite faith in the technological fix, the guarantee of everything coming out right.

> If something bad happens to us, we are outraged because our lives are supposed to be perfect. Two generations ago, if infants were born with birth defects, it was considered an act of God or an act of nature. Today if the baby is not absolutely perfect, the tendency is to believe the doctor is responsible. We've created a set of social expectations and a legal structure in which the blame game can be played as never before. (Blackman, Curry, Reingold, "Crybabies: Eternal Victims," *Time)*

At the other end of the life span, we are now demanding a gentle death as our constitutional right. There is a push for euthanasia laws allowing doctors to end life prematurely if it looks like it will cost too much suffering. Legal or not, some doctors do it anyway; Dr. Kevorkian's "suicide machine" is the most infamous example.

A Liberating Insight

What does all this have to do with ecology? Just this: Deep within all of us is *the assumption that we know best what the world is for and how earthly life ought to be.* We imagine that it is all under our control and we have the final say.

The illusion of control over the ultimate areas of birth and death is only a logical extension of the illusion of control over nature. And as we've already seen, the lust for power to define and use natural forces is the same egoism seen in people on *all* sides of ecological controversies, from proponents of "unlimited growth" to disciples of "the simple life."

11

The realization that *all* discussion of ecology is affected by the same human flaws is very liberating to Christians concerned for the environment. It means we are free to read and listen to arguments from all different sides of the issues. It means we do not have to swallow whole—nor reject automatically—any opinion by any writer because of a particular position on the environmental spectrum. We can study and learn from all of it, knowing it is all potentially instructive and useful (though all imperfect). That's why the pile of material on our desk keeps landsliding onto the floor. That's why it will get even larger and more varied before this project is over.

Realizing that all discussion of ecology is humanly flawed is liberating in another way. It means we do not have to pretend that *our* present view of ecology is the last word. Our ideas are free to grow and change. We have another, final Word—the Word revealed in Christ and Scripture—by which to evaluate any ideas about ecology, including our own ideas. We do not have to defend the ideas and actions of all Christians as though they were always right. If we look at history and find that Christians have sometimes defied God in their relationship with his creation, we don't have to toss out the whole Christian faith, and neither do we have to justify those people's actions just because they identified themselves as Christians.

The most famous example in American history sits in the hot seat right now. The 500th anniversary of Christopher Columbus's voyages is coming up, and we're working on this book during the heat of the controversy. When we tell people about our project, they often say "What about Columbus?" and challenge us about European exploitation of the "New World."

So far we've run into nothing like the picket line that confronted Susan Milbrath, a Florida museum curator, at the opening of her Columbus Quincentennial exhibit.

Milbrath's response? She wanted to know why people concentrate only on the sins of Columbus and the Spanish conquerors. She asked, "The big question to me is, are *human beings* good?" (Cerio, "The Black Legend: Were the Spaniards that Cruel?" *Newsweek*).

A good question. Realizing the human flaw in all ecological discussions means we must confess our own guilt for the state of the earth (true guilt, not externally imposed guiltiness). The ecological problem is the natural result of our refusal to live as created beings under the authority and care of a Creator. Of that, we are all guilty.

Dissatisfaction = hope

The illusion that nature is *ours* to define and use as we want naturally leaves people chronically dissatisfied. And as long as a person is dissatisfied, there is always hope. Dissatisfaction means we think things can be better. Unless we are fatalists, lack of satisfaction leads us to look for other alternatives. But as Walter Shapiro wrote, "Until something new replaces it, materialism will in some way fill the void" (Shapiro, "The Birth and—Maybe—Death of Yuppiedom," *Time*).

Christian faith is exactly that "something new" that can fill the void. It is "the old, old story," but it is also new to each new believer, and it brings renewed hope to us when problems seem overwhelming.

Christ offers an alternative to the self-protective guarding of lifestyles.

Christ offers a revolutionary alternative vision of the Good Life.

And Christ offers a holy standard, beyond ourselves, for defining nature and determining the right use of the earth.

Our aim in this book is not to be guilt-inducing but hope-inspiring. But before we consider our hope for the future, let's look at how we got to this point of imagining that the earth is ours to use as we wish.

CHAPTER TWO
HOW WE GOT HERE

It is entirely in keeping with man's feeling about nature
that when he suddenly notices his drinking fountain losing pressure,
he should ascend to heaven and beat a cloud over the ears.
E.B. White, "Rainmakers"

When I (Sandy) lived at home, it was before the age of hand-held blow-dryers. When I washed my hair in winter, I would dry it by sitting in front of the draft from the wall register in my room. The house was tight, and the thermostat would shut off the furnace promptly— before my hair was dry. So I would keep turning up the thermostat and the hot air would keep blowing out not only my register but all the registers. I was using a six-room house for a hair dryer.

Though I was raised with a deep appreciation for nature and was not encouraged to waste things, I never thought to make any connection between depleting natural gas resources and my convenient hair-drying arrangement. Actually, it wasn't so convenient, jumping up and turning up the thermostat every few minutes. But it made perfect sense at the time.

If I'd had any idea that someday I would be writing a book on ecology (or, for that matter, if I had been paying the gas bill) I would never have done that. I tell the story to show that wastefulness is perfectly logical, if only you adopt the attitude that natural resources are there to be used and we have the right to use all we want.

Inconsistent Living

In recent years several "media star" Christians have fallen from their high places after being caught in sexual sin. Comedians and journalists had a field day scoffing at the scandals. Their scorn is interesting, because you would expect them to react more like this: "Well, good, those Christians have finally come out of the Victorian Age and joined the real world." After all, the behavior they sneer at is considered normal and acceptable in non-Christian society. But behind the jokes and accusations is the remnant of a moral base, the assumption that those people *ought* to have lived by righteous standards.

Then why didn't they? The specific reasons vary from case to case, but somehow God and sexuality must have gotten separated in those people's minds. The spiritual and the physical were compartmentalized; the ways of God could be preached from the pulpit while simultaneously ignored in private life. Despite what the person *said,* he *acted* as though God were nowhere around. The result was disaster for both those who did the wrong and all who trusted them.

The "separation" principle goes beyond sexuality. Any time we divorce God from any aspect of life, that area becomes wide open for selfish exploitation, to the hurt of both the exploited and the exploiter. It's as true in our relations with the earth as in our relations with other people.

Divorcing life from morality
Using anything so casually—whether another person or the energy reserves beneath the ground—requires first making certain presumptions.

We must presume that we have both the *ability* and the *right* to exploit the object of our desire. Our thinking cannot be cluttered with any voices telling us we *cannot* or *should not* do what we please with the exploited object. Such a world view demands a certain inflated picture of ourselves: filled with power and rights, free of limits on abilities or morals.

In short, *in order to exploit anything freely we must imagine ourselves living in a universe divorced from a moral God who made us and has ultimate say in how we live.* We must inhabit (or rather think we inhabit) a closed system from which God is excluded.

Now we want to ask when and where in our own history, the history of Western culture, such a divorce between God and the world came about, when humans began to imagine that they lived in a universe where God was not actively involved.

A History of a World View

Medieval and Renaissance views of God and humanity
For our direct cultural ancestors, life was not always divorced from God. In the medieval period in Europe, nature provided unquestionable evidence of God's existence, care, love, and righteous judgment. The world's grand design and hierarchy of being spoke of One who made and ruled all creation. All things, from worm to rock to humankind to star, were engaged in a celestial dance that glorified the Creator. In the cycle of seasons and the threat of disease and early death, people could not escape their daily dependence on their Maker for food, health, and safety.

People looked to the church to tell them who they were and where they fit in the unalterable scheme of things. At that time "to praise man was to praise God, for man was a creation of God." In the blossoming of the Renaissance, God was still seen as the Lord who acted in this world, but "writers praised man himself as a creator."

They played down the sinfulness he was born with and emphasized his ability to think and act for himself, to produce works of art, to guide the destiny of others. They freed man from his pegged place in the medieval hierarchy, halfway between matter

17

and spirit, and allowed him to roam at will, through all levels of being, sometimes identifying himself with the brutes, sometimes with the angels. He was seen as the ruler of nature—the lord, although not the Lord, of creation. (Hale, *Renaissance,* pp. 17-18)

In the period of the Renaissance, people began looking beyond the church and asking about the world and their place in it. The fifteenth century brought the invention of the printing press, the nautical compass, and gunpowder (imported from the East). It was also a time of world exploration that enormously expanded the perceived limits of human activity. Human will and passion showed in a new artistic naturalism, a celebration of humanity, though its expression was often turned to the service of the church.

The new emphasis on individuality and freedom set the stage for the Reformation. Now each person could come to God directly and be forgiven by the grace of Christ through faith alone. For the Reformers every person was responsible before God, every believer a priest, the way to God open to everyone by faith, and the Bible an open book to any literate person.

Although an authoritarian church no longer held full authority over human activities, the Reformers saw this world as the arena of God's redeeming activity, a place to be brought increasingly under the lordship of Christ. Martin Luther even spoke of looking at the natural world with a more sensitive and appreciative eye: "We now look deeper into creation than we did under the papacy. They used to pass it by, looking at nature with the interest of a cow" (Simon, *The Reformation,* p. 173). The Reformers knew that God was ever-present in his world with life-giving grace.

But already the doors of the Western mind were closing, swinging shut on the well-oiled hinges of the great universal Machine.

The Age of Reason

A new world view was spreading across Europe. It was human-centered, based on natural reason, thoroughly trusting of empirical observation and conclusions drawn by rational and (in the opinion of some) perfectible humans. Naturally it was cynical and skeptical about orthodox religion.

We can hear some of the first creaking of the hinges around 1600 when Francis Bacon wrote a proposed renovation of the sciences, saying that Nature is best observed once it is bent by the human hand. His greatest work, *Novum Organum* (1620), sets forth the experimental method of science. In it Bacon complained that the rise of Christianity had turned "by far the greater number of the best wits" toward theology and religious controversies and away from scientific inquiry *(Novum Organum,* in *The English Philosophers,* p. 55).

Francis Bacon could not let go of God because the experimental method is possible only in an *orderly* universe where experiments replicate themselves. The Christian world view, which holds to a God who created an orderly natural world and keeps it running according to observable laws, is what makes natural science possible.

Bacon had faith that humanity would use science wisely: "Only let the human race recover the right over nature which belongs to it by divine bequest," he wrote, "and let power be given it; the exercise thereof will be governed by sound reason and true religion" (ibid., 86).

Isaac Newton continued the reshaping of science. Scientific method, based on drawing conclusions from observable phenomena, came to be applied not only to the natural sciences but to government, law, economics, theology, ethics, morality, and human nature itself.

Whether the human race really has a "right over nature which belongs to it by divine bequest" as Bacon said, we will consider further. For now what matters is to see that as Enlightenment thinking spread across Europe, such a supposed human power and right was divorced from its Giver and was interpreted as *the right to exploit nature for all it could give.* A growing cadre of "philosophes"—radical scholars and intellectuals—set out to secularize life and close tight the doors of the universe against any miraculous or moral interference.

Enlightenment and the utopian dream

"The utopian dream of the Enlightenment," Francis Schaeffer summarized, "can be summed up by five words: reason, nature, happiness, progress, and liberty. It was thoroughly secular in its thinking. The humanistic elements which had risen during the Renaissance came to flood tide in the Enlightenment. Here was man starting from himself absolutely" (Schaeffer, *How Should We Then Live?* p. 121).

Gifted writers such as Voltaire mocked Christian faith with cynicism and wit. If there is no such thing as the miraculous, if there is no living God active in human affairs, then obviously Christian faith is ridiculous, because it believes in miracles and an active God.

The Enlightenment philosophers often disagreed with one another, writes historian Peter Gay, but the one thing this "impressive clan of radical intellectuals" had in common was "a critical attitude toward any sort of orthodoxy, and especially toward orthodox religion" (Gay, *Age of Enlightenment,* p. 11).

Perhaps Christianity was deemed ridiculous because it threatened the world view the "philosophes" preferred, since they

> contemplated Nature in all her manifestations, but always in relation to Man: they were cosmic philosophers, but they never doubted that Nature was to be judged by her usefulness to Man, and their theologians stood ready to prove that every phenomenon of Nature was designed by Providence for the convenience of Man. (Commager, *The Empire of Reason,* pp. 42-43)

If nature exists solely for the benefit of humanity and is only waiting passively for us to extract its riches, then a personal God who might interfere with the process—and who might demand accountability for it—is a nuisance and an impediment to progress. If humankind is the measure of everything, there is no room for a faith that dares to say of Jesus Christ that "all things were created by him and for him" (Col. 1:16) and that "at the name of Jesus every knee should bow, in heaven and on earth and under the earth" (Phil. 2:10).

Writing God out of the formula

So in the Age of Reason, God was a problem standing in the way of human development. Of course he could be denied as nonexistent, but it's difficult to prove scientifically the nonexistence of anything. There was a more comfortable alternative for getting the Deity out of the way—a method that gave people room to enjoy their God-given freedom under a benign Providence but without his interference.

The Age of Reason disposed of God in an ingeniously religious way. "If these men had a religion," Francis Schaeffer wrote, "it was deism" (Schaeffer, *How Should We Then Live?* p. 121).

Deism was the religion that got God out of the way. Deism recognizes a Creator God, but its God is a master mechanic who long ago wound up the universe and left it to run in its self-contained system while he distanced himself.

A short definition of deism in contemporary language might describe it as the conception that God has created the world in such a perfect manner that immediately afterwards he could afford to go into early retirement. The God of deism, in fact, has often been compared with a clockmaker, a superior technician and mathematician, who is capable of making such a perfect timepiece that once it is set in motion, it no longer needs his further attention. . . . It is this natural law, therefore, which *replaces God* and executes the role of providence in the world. (Goudzwaard, *Capitalism and Progress,* pp. 20-21, emphasis added)

With this mechanistic view, it logically followed that "the only reliable road to knowledge of God's plans was through science, not religion, through observation and experiment, not dogma and revelation" (Gay, *Age of Enlightenment,* p. 12).

The religion called "progress"

In the Middle Ages, the church had told people who they were and where they fit in the scheme of things. The Renaissance and Reformation had freed people from an authoritarian church, but they still lived under the hand of Providence. Now *Progress became Providence*. Perfectible and free from the demands of a righteous God, humanity was engaged in an inevitable upward climb, unrestrained by limits on "can" or "should." A moral God demanding justice was replaced by an invisible hand guaranteeing progress.

Mechanistic natural law providing for unstoppable progress was the basis of Adam Smith's economics as developed in *The Wealth of Nations*. For Smith the only value was human labor as humanity struggles to elicit goods from nature—a struggle that can only lead to progress. Of course that is a very mechanistic view of human sweat. Smith defended total economic freedom and insisted that there would always be enough for rich and poor alike: "The rich consume little more than the poor . . . [thus led] by an invisible hand to make nearly the same distribution of the necessaries of life, which would have been made, had the earth been divided into equal portions among all its inhabitants; and thus, without intending it, without knowing it advanced the interest of society" (quoted in Goudzwaard, *Capitalism*, p. 25).

John Stuart Mill agreed with Smith. If there were too many people in the world and therefore not enough food to go around, it was because nature was not generous enough in giving up its bounty to human work. "The niggardliness of nature, not the injustice of society, is the cause of the penalty attached to overpopulation" (Mill, *Principles of Political Economy*, p. 191).

Unexpected Results

The conception of Nature as only a machine, and the "freeing" of nature from God, led logically to the loosing of all controls over how humans made use of that machine. There were no longer limits on "can" or "should." It is that philosophical divorce that brought—and still brings—tragedy to the exploited and the exploiters.

The tragedy was not obvious at first. Initially, the divorce looked riotously optimistic. Humanity would solve its problems by reason. In France, revolutionaries "proclaimed the goddess of Reason in Notre-Dame Cathedral in Paris and in other churches. . . . In Paris, the goddess was personified by an actress, Demoiselle Candeille, carried shoulder-high into the cathedral by men dressed in Roman costumes" (Schaeffer, *How Should We Then Live?* p. 38). But the triumph of "Reason" in the French Revolution led many to unreasonable deaths. Confined to his cell, the Marquis de Condorcet, former chairman of the French Legislative Assembly, wrote a "Sketch for a Historical Picture of the Progress of the Human Mind." His writing is a vision of progress, of man's victory over nature and the perfectibility of man. Shortly after writing it, he was guillotined in the madness of the French Revolution.

Caught in our own machine

And so God was relegated to the status of a benevolent being who was necessary to get the world going and keep it running smoothly, but who otherwise had no business intervening in things. It's a view of God still held informally by many of us.

We can trace many of today's comforts and political freedoms to the Enlightenment period of scientific inquiry, social revolution, and technological inventiveness. But because it was coupled with the closing off of nature from God, it all has come at a high price.

Throughout the Renaissance and the Enlightenment, people looked for a unified system of knowledge that would give life meaning. At first the reduction of the universe to a machine promised an answer: If nature was a machine operating by natural law in a closed system, it should be possible to find a unified system of truth to explain life. Meaning came in the very effort to find meaning, to understand this mechanistic system.

But there was a problem. Separating nature from God produces a sense of pseudo-freedom and pseudo-power, but it leads to consequences we can't live with. If the universe is nothing but a machine, and humanity is not outside the universe, then we are all part of the machine. In essence that was the title of Julien de la Mettrie's book, *L'homme machine.* Humankind therefore cannot be ruler of the machine; we are only another cog within it.

Human reason, which had promised power and freedom, now brought us to the conclusion that we are merely part of the machine; life is without meaning. But of course we cannot live sanely thinking we are only machines. Human beings are more than flesh and blood. We are made to hope; we cannot live with the logical results of our Enlightenment reasonableness.

It may seem that we have wandered far afield from ecology, but there is a connection.

The coming of despair

Just when Western society was becoming conscious of an environmental crisis, Francis Schaeffer wrote an analysis of humanity's loss of hope. Reason without God, he said, has led to living below a "line of despair." Twentieth-century people have dealt with that sense of despair by existentialism. We acknowledge that there is no meaning but declare that, by taking action, we can give life meaning. Above the "line" hangs a tantalizing nonrational hope. Despair thus leads to unreasonable action, doing things in an attempt to inject meaning into life, an existential "leap of faith."

> In other words, in the lower story, on the basis of all reason, man as man is dead. You have simply mathematics, particulars, mechanics. Man has no meaning, no purpose, no significance. There is only pessimism concerning man as man. But up above, on the basis of a non-rational, non-reasonable leap, there is a non-reasonable faith which gives optimism. This is modern man's total dichotomy. (Schaeffer, *Escape from Reason,* pp. 46-47)

No wonder we expend so much energy defending lifestyles that don't really satisfy us or give us meaning! So many of us are living in a closed-system universe where God has no intimate everyday involvement—and no say in our decisions. The result is the chronic emptiness we talked about in the preceding chapter.

In search of meaning
If we find life empty, how will we try to fill it? Many with an economic orientation to things instead of persons try to find meaning by turning to materialism—craving, producing, and then throwing away material goods only to crave more.

No wonder we overuse and abuse the earth. Why not? If taking action in the here and now is all that can give us meaning, why not live for all the pleasure possible here and now? There are no moral limits ("should"), so our only limits are our technical abilities ("can") and they are expanding every day.

If nature is a machine to be exploited and humanity sets the rules, there are no limits on ecological destruction.

We are talking about the historical results of the European Enlightenment because we are talking about the roots of our own culture. We do not need to absorb all the blame (though some try to throw it all our way). Ours is not the only society to abuse the natural world. But we must understand our own history in order to see how we got to this place of abusing nature in a futile chase to satisfy ourselves—and how God got edited out of the equation.

Running out of resources
Enlightenment rationalism held sway as long as there was apparently enough of everything and "we" were in control of nature. But the environmental crisis has challenged all that. Nature is no longer so benignly cooperative in our use of it.

Jeremy Rifkin wrote that "Faith in the liberating power of materialism carries with it one critical assumption, the belief that the earth possesses unlimited abundance" (Rifkin, *The Emerging Order: God in the Age of Scarcity,* p. 25). But the earth is apparently no longer yielding more than can possibly be used. Instead, humanity's lordship over nature is apparently producing disaster. Over the past twenty years the evidence has been pouring in, and it threatens everyone, especially those of us in comfortable Western industrialized societies who thought our resources were unlimited and our power was unstoppable.

As our cherished assumptions and presuppositions fall away, we face a crisis of faith.

> The theme of progress has penetrated western society so profoundly because it was able to present itself as a faith in progress, as a religion of progress. That is also why the present-day crisis of the idea of progress has the depth of a crisis of faith. There is more at stake than a somewhat reduced confidence in "progress" on the part of western man. His whole life perspective has undergone a shock. (Goudzwaard, *Capitalism & Progress,* p. 248)

What do we do in the face of this crisis, which is as much philosophical as physical? There are many theories, but they can be reduced to two main streams, as the next chapter will show.

CHAPTER THREE
TWO POPULAR VIEWS

Two roads diverged in a wood, and I—
I took the one less traveled by,
And that has made all the difference.
Robert Frost, "The Road Not Taken"

The wild horse, free-spirited symbol of the American West, was once endangered by "mustangers" (as in "The Misfits") who ran them down and rounded them up for sale. After legislation was passed in 1971 to protect the horses on federal lands, they multiplied so quickly that they soon competed with cattle and sheep for grazing land on the range.

Two researchers hit on a scheme to control the wild horse population. "Until now," wrote one, "there have been just two decidedly unscientific ways to deal with proliferating 'mustangs':. . . kill them or round them up for adoption." John W. Turner, Jr., and Jay Kirkpatrick found another solution. Using a dart-firing rifle, they injected the more dominant stallions with an anti-fertility drug that lasted through one breeding season. Turner explained, "The drugging approach constitutes a scientific option that is cheaper, easier and far more humane than the other two."

However, the government balked at continuing to provide funds for the project. Turner wrote, "Fiscal prudence suggests that after years of harassment we owe these doughty animals _the kind of genuine freedom that only applied science can deliver_" (Turner, "Given a Free Rein, Prolific Mustangs Gallop into Trouble," _Smithsonian_, emphasis added).

The wild horse birth-control program is an excellent example of a technological approach to an environmental problem. It is humans intervening in the natural order, and it gets the job done efficiently. It keeps the horses from being shot or sold into captivity, but it also reflects the economic judgment that wild horses, which do not "pay," must yield their numbers to cattle and sheep, which do "pay."

Two Approaches

We Americans have always been ingenious at finding technological solutions to problems, and many of us would like to believe the environmental crisis will be no different. Others mistrust technology and are calling for a deeper revision of basic values.

Out of all the voices telling us what we should do about the ecological crisis, these are the two main strands we discern: the human-centered (we'll call it the _technological_) and the nature-centered (we'll call it the _mystical_).

It's important to realize right at the start that the differences between the human-centered and the nature-centered approaches are not over what _can_ be done. They differ at their core over what _should_ be done. They are two divergent ethics reflecting two very different views of reality.

Two kinds of environmental ethic are possible. The obvious kind is anthropocentric. Right and wrong are determined by human interest. This ethic (let us call it the humanistic ethic) is secondarily an environmental ethic; concern for the environment is entirely subsidiary to a concern for _humans,_ who are helped or hurt by the

_28_

condition of their surroundings. (Rolston, *Philosophy Gone Wild,* p. 145)

Human-Centered: Onward and Upward

Whether you call it human-centered, technological, or anthropocentric, this view is relentlessly optimistic. If there is an ecological crisis—and some even say there isn't—then it has been caused by human inventiveness and ingenuity gone somewhat misguided. The cure is more and better human inventiveness and ingenuity. Even problems that have been caused by technology can be solved by more technology. We should not be ashamed of our science and industry or look at human marks on the earth as scars, says this view. We humans have always reshaped the earth and benefited from the reshaping, and we will continue to do so.

A recent book by E. Calvin Beisner, *Prospects for Growth,* is an excellent and well-written example of the technological view. Beisner describes the relationship between nature and humanity in these terms:

It is not the earth that provides what human beings demand. In fact, aside from a marginally adequate biosphere, the earth provides us with very little. . . . It is man's mind operating through his body—both gifts of God—that provides most of what man wants and needs as he reshapes, reconstitutes, and recombines what he finds in nature. (Beisner, *Prospects for Growth: A Biblical View of Population, Resources, and the Future,* pp. 62-63)

A *Newsweek* cover story on "Cleaning Up Our Mess" had very little to say about the value of nature for nature's sake; instead it delved into legal and technological solutions for efficiently cleaning up our waste. Even its rationale for saving endangered plant and animal species was that we might someday need them in the lab. "Who can say whether man, as he learns genetic engineering, won't need to reach into some obscure subspecies and pluck out DNA that helps him endure some coming ecological transition, perhaps one of his own making?" (Easterbrook, "Cleaning Up," *Newsweek).*

Nature redesigned

You may find the human-centered view of nature arrogant, but you can't call it pessimistic. It is unfailingly upbeat about humanity as well as about nature.

While acknowledging that wilderness gives us a sense of awe and makes us realize our smallness in the cosmos, the prominent scientist Rene Dubos finds truest beauty and harmony in the "humanization of the earth." Far from ruining everything, he says, the human race has actually improved things.

> I admire the high Alps, the Sierras, the Himalayas, but my love extends to less grandiose sceneries structured by human intelligence and imbued with the human presence. . . . Earth has potentialities that remain unexpressed until properly manipulated by human labor and imagination. (Dubos, *The Wooing of Earth,* pp. xiv-xv)

A tree-farm manager, daughter of a logger and married to a logger, asks us to compare the scenic value of a "natural" forest with a "managed" one. In the forest untouched by human influence, the hiker is met with unsightly "old trees, the dead and dying trees, the windfalls crisscrossing the forest." In the managed forest, "one sees the older stands with the forest floor cleared of the dead windfalls, leaving a more parklike setting." "True environmentalists," she goes on to say, "husband the land; they do not let the crops stagnate and rot" (Kyser, "A Logger's Lament," *Newsweek).*

Conquering the land

Even die-hard lovers of wilderness must acknowledge the nobility and triumph with which humanity sometimes leaves its mark on that wilderness. In his beautiful book *The Necessity of Empty Places,*

Paul Gruchow treks to various wild spots throughout Nebraska and Wyoming. Invading nature's spaces, so to speak, he is enchanted by the beauty and mystery of their existence remote from humans.

Then Gruchow visits Independence Rock, a milestone for the wagon trains on the Oregon Trail. Vicariously he feels "the relief, the momentary rush of calm, the excitement, of turning around the bend in the valley and seeing the rock and knowing that you were two-fifths of the way West and all was well."

The rock is a registry of the way west. Travelers memorialized their arrival by writing their names and the date on the rock in charcoal or paint, or by scratching or carving or chiseling. Gruchow would be expected to resent their human graffiti desecrating the natural landscape. But as he climbs the rock and imagines the smoke of campfires and the cry of the wagonmaster, he is deeply moved by the human element of "defiance and pride, determination and hope, resignation and prayer" superimposed upon nature.

I saw in those names the beginnings of many other names, of a new generation of names born in the West, the names of mountains, of lakes and streams, of fledgling towns, of roads and passes, of children born along the trail, or on new farms, or in mining camps, and destined to make of a wide and nameless place a new and richly designated one. (Gruchow, *The Necessity of Empty Places,* pp. 275-276)

Christians have no problem with a noble view of humanity. The Bible tells us we are higher than animals or rocks or trees. "You made him a little lower than the heavenly beings and crowned him with glory and honor. You made him ruler over the works of your hands; you put everything under his feet" (Ps. 8:5-6). "Look at the birds of the air . . . Are you not much more valuable than they?" (Matt. 6:26).

That is not *all* the Bible has to say about humanity's condition, but it is *part* of what it says. As we'll see more fully in Chapter 7, we are not the leftovers of God's creation. Who can deny that humankind has done great things and is always looking for greater things to do? As Carl Sandburg said in *The People, Yes* (1936), "The people take the earth as a tomb of rest and a cradle of hope. . . . In the night, and overhead a shovel of stars for keeps, the people march. 'Where to? What next?' "

At odds with economics

With all it has to commend it, the technological approach to environmental problems has its limitations. A major limitation is that it carries on a running conflict with economics. As ecological problems are identified and solutions formed, economic interests surface to challenge them.

Atlantic Richfield recently developed a cleaner-burning gasoline that it claims will cut toxic emissions by 50 percent. *Time* magazine asked, "If making a better gasoline is so easy, why hasn't anyone done it before? The simple answer: cleaner fuels are more expensive" (Elmer-DeWitt, "Gee, Your Car Smells Terrific!" *Time*). When cost meets ecology, cost frequently wins.

After the Environmental Protection Agency was founded in 1970, it was soon tangled in legal battles over proving what levels of pollution really were unacceptable. Accused polluters could always say that there wasn't enough evidence yet for acid rain or auto emissions or smokestack standards. Industry could delay nearly any proposed regulation "simply by trotting out an expert who would testify that further study was required" (Easterbrook, "Cleaning Up," *Newsweek*).

Polluters naturally balk at spending money on the environment unless absolutely necessary—that is, until forced. The technological approach cooperates with their reluctance because it is the nature of science always to demand more proof.

A physicist writing in *Smithsonian* magazine explains why skeptics cast doubt on such concepts as the "greenhouse effect" (global warming caused by gases in the atmosphere) and "nuclear winter" (worldwide freezing after a nuclear war). Such frightening scenarios are based on computer models, which in turn are based on certain assumptions that may be suspect. "We are going to face serious problems" in the twenty-first century, he says, "and we will have to face them while the scientific evidence for the seriousness (and even the existence) of the problems is clouded by doubt and controversy" (Trefil, "Modeling Earth's Future Climate Requires Both Science and Guesswork," *Smithsonian*).

Nature-Centered: Equal Rights

The nature-centered environmental ethic avoids the difficult demands of either scientific proof or economics. It rests on wholly different ground—just *how* different, we're going to explore.

> The naturalistic ethic, held perhaps more intensely by fewer advocates, is directly about *nature*. It holds that some natural objects, like whooping cranes, are morally considerable in their own right, apart from human interests, or that some ecosystems, perhaps the Great Smokies, have intrinsic values, such as aesthetic beauty, from which we derive a duty to respect these landscapes. (Rolston, *Philosophy Gone Wild,* p. 145)

Rolston understated his case. Holders of the naturalistic ethic do not limit it to "some" animals like whooping cranes or "some" ecosystems like the Great Smokies. They see all of Nature as having rights equal to humanity's.

In Jeremy Bentham's utilitarian ethics, the rightness or wrongness of an act is determined by the degree to which it causes pleasure or pain. Color of skin does not exempt a person from the right to avoid pain, and he wondered whether the day might come when the number of legs, skin, and spinal cord would also be irrelevant. "The question is not, Can they *reason?* nor Can they *talk?*, but Can they *suffer?*" (Bentham, *An Introduction to the Principles of Morals and Legislation,* quoted in Nash, *The Rights of Nature,* p. 23).

Popular thought has not only caught up with Bentham's question but has gone beyond it. In recent decades the concept of "rights" has been expanding to include the rights of animals, plants, inanimate objects, the earth, the solar system, and the universe. Roderick Frazier Nash calls this the natural expansion of a circle of rights that has been widening since the Enlightenment.

When the Declaration of Independence proclaimed the inalienable rights to "life, liberty, and the pursuit of happiness," certain persons were excluded from those rights, notably African slaves, Indians, and to some extent white women. Gradually more and more rights were extended (by law and social change) to more and more humans. Now, says Nash, the circle is expanding to include animals, plants, and inanimate objects—in other words, all of nature (Nash, *The Rights of Nature: A History of Environmental Ethics,* p. 7).

The "land ethic"

In 1949, Wisconsin writer Aldo Leopold proposed a "land ethic" as a logical extension of prior ethics. The first ethics, he said, dealt with the relation between individuals; later additions to ethics dealt with the relation between the individual and society. The further expansion to land, he said, is only logical:

> The land ethic simply enlarges the boundaries of the community to include soils, waters, plants, and animals, or collectively: the land. . . . In short, a land ethic changes the role of *Homo sapiens* from conqueror of the land-community to plain member and citizen of it. (Leopold, *A Sand County Almanac,* p. 204)

Recently a temporary tragedy happened at the Sigurd Olson Environmental Institute up the street from us. Sig Olson's antique canoe disappeared from its place bolted fourteen feet up on an interior wall. A mysterious letter appeared revealing where the canoe was hidden in the attic of another building on campus, and the canoe, symbolic of the Institute, was restored.

For many years Sig Olson canoed and hiked and fished and hunted throughout the United States, but he retained his special love for the Lake Superior region of cold water, loon calls in the night, pungent spruce, and whitetail deer. "The real importance of this region I know so well," he wrote, "is not the vast deposits of minerals and timber or the part they play in our economy; the real importance lies in the values we find there and that we take with us when we leave, although we may not quite understand them" (Olson, *Of Time and Place*, p. 4).

Sig Olson had this to say of the concept of a "land ethic:"

> A land ethic is a philosophical point of view involved with morality and character. . . . We ask ourselves if we are doing what is right. Are we good stewards? Have we done all we could to stop ugliness, devastation, and decay in the world around us? If the answer is yes, then we have embraced what is meant by a land ethic. (Ibid., 167)

The natural "mystique"

Many people feel that the time is here for revising our view of the relationship of humanity to nature. They call for a concept more mystical than "stewardship."

In 1970, a British editorialist wrote that the basis of Western ethics would have to be completely revised before Aldo Leopold's "land ethic" would ever be adopted. The idea of extending ethics to include the land "could not be carried into effect, that Western ethics would have to be *not extended but abandoned*. . . . In search of such an ecological approach, he tells us, men will turn in vain to a Western-type ethic, however extended. They will need to look, rather, to 'Hindu and Buddhist faiths . . . or the peasant cultures of Asia'" (Passmore, *Man's Responsibility for Nature*, p. 4, emphasis added).

Environmentalists *have* looked Eastward and to "aboriginal" cultures that apparently live in greater harmony with the land. They have also looked inward to their own souls for answers.

What many people are demanding is not an improved technology but a radically new *faith*—a reuniting of what the Age of Reason split apart: nature and God. They are calling for a theology of the earth—a faith that will bring back balance and harmony between humanity and nature, a faith that will give hope, a faith that will save us. We can call this the *mystical* view.

Aboriginal ideals

People are realizing that more primitive cultures lived (and in some places still live) in closer harmony with the earth than we do in our technology-encased existence. That is the reason for the tremendous surge in interest in native American and other "aboriginal" cultures, not to study them as oddities but to learn from them and adopt some of their ways. *Sojourners* magazine devoted an entire issue to "1992: Rediscovering America" (October 1991). With the 500th anniversary of Columbus's landing comes a call for massive repentance of the damage done to the native peoples by the waves of European invaders.

In many environmental circles the native American is looked to as the ideal of living in harmony with the earth. Our Pilgrim Fathers would have starved, they point out, if Indians had not showed them how to live here. *Sesame Street Magazine* offers children a revisionist view of the first Thanksgiving:

> The first Thanksgiving feast took place a very long time ago, in 1621. The Native Americans joined the Pilgrims for a special meal. The Pilgrims were thankful for all the food that the American Indians had helped them grow that year. They ate fruit, cornbread, turkey, and pies. What do you eat at Thanksgiving?

Earth a goddess

We're familiar now with the image of the whole earth, cloud-swirled and suspended in blackness. But if you remember seeing it for the first time broadcast from Apollo 8, you know what a stunning and deeply moving sight it was. For the first time we stepped back and took a look at ourselves—only to find we could not see ourselves at all.

David Brinkley remarked at the time that the earth looked pretty much like Rand McNally's maps always said it did. But in another way it did not look like Rand McNally at all. Most of the things we memorized in geography class were invisible. The lines and labels, the human-made boundaries and names, were missing. In fact, there was no visible evidence of humanity; there was only the incredibly beautiful planet.

Who wasn't deeply moved when the astronauts read the creation story from Genesis 1 and sent back the Christmas message, "God bless all of you—all of you on the good earth"?

Time changes the interpretation of events. Now, according to James Lovelock and others, that look back over our shoulder at ourselves was the work of the living organism Gaia, self-regulating for eons, becoming at last self-conscious.

James Lovelock was a prestigious English scientist who invented the electron capture detector (ECD) to measure the buildup of chlorofluorocarbon gases in the earth's atmosphere that are apparently depleting the ozone layer. In the late 1960s he began to be intrigued by the idea that the earth is one entity constituting a self-regulating system that seeks and maintains its own optimal environment. That's in sharp contrast to the traditional evolutionary view that life on earth is the chance product of adaptation to the environment.

This theoretical planet-sized entity needed a name, which was provided by Lovelock's neighbor, the novelist William Golding (who wrote *Lord of the Flies*). Golding suggested "Gaia," the Greek earth goddess whose name is at the root of *geography* and *geology.*

In 1969 Lovelock first put forth the Gaia hypothesis. He expected (hoped) to be condemned by the church as Galileo had been, but as he wryly remarks, "It is the scientific establishment that now forbids heresy." His scientific colleagues, not the church, rose up in anger. "I had a faint hope that *Gaia* might be denounced from the pulpit; instead I was asked to deliver a sermon on *Gaia* at the cathedral of St. John the Divine in New York" (Lovelock, *Gaia: A New Look at Life on Earth*, p. vii).

Despite the compelling imagery of Gaia as a living goddess figure, Lovelock attempted to keep his scientific credibility by depersonalizing her: "Occasionally it has been difficult . . . to avoid talking of Gaia as if she were known to be sentient. This is meant no more seriously than is the appellation 'she' when given to a ship by those who sail in her" (ibid., xii). However, by the end of that book Lovelock was musing: "If we are a part of Gaia it becomes interesting to ask: 'To what extent is our collective intelligence also a part of Gaia? Do we as a species constitute a Gaian nervous system and a brain which can consciously anticipate environmental changes?'" (ibid., 147).

"Deep ecology"

The term *deep ecology* was coined by Arne Naess, professor of philosophy at Oslo University in Norway, in 1973 to go "beyond a limited piecemeal shallow approach to environmental problems and attempt to articulate *a comprehensive religious and philosophical worldview*" (Devall and Sessions, *Deep Ecology: Living As If Nature Mattered*, p. 65, emphasis added).

> "Deep ecology" differs from "environmentalism" . . . less by its position on any given policy or crisis than by its way of envisioning *what it means to be human,* and how humans should relate to other forms of being. . . . The issue is important because, if human beings are not superior to other life forms, then human considerations are not privileged in forming moral judgments. (Richards, "The Nature-Culture Dilemma," *Breakthrough*, emphasis added)

Naess wished to reorient ethics by enlarging our concept of *self* "to include ever wider reaches of life, embracing, finally, all of being and the bonds which hold everything together in an ever-expanding universe." He claimed he did not mean to confuse such expansion of the self with Eastern mysticism, which loses the self in mystical union with the whole; he also saw diversity and individuality as essential for good ecology (ibid., 9). Naess's followers, however, have failed to make the distinction.

Deep ecology has two "ultimate norms," that is, two unquestionable "intuitions which are themselves not derivable from other principles or intuitions." They are *self-realization* and *biocentric equality.*

Self-realization. The first "ultimate norm," self-realization, seems at first glance to have nothing to do with ecology. In fact it would seem to work against it. Self-centeredness would appear to be at the heart of abusing anything, including the earth. However, deep ecology's "self-realization"

> goes beyond the modern Western self which is defined as an isolated ego. . . . Spiritual growth, or unfolding, begins when we cease to understand or see ourselves as isolated and narrow competing egos and begin to identify with other humans from our family and friends to, eventually, our species. But the deep ecology sense of self requires a further maturity and growth, an identification which goes beyond humanity to include the nonhuman world. (Devall and Sessions, *Deep Ecology,* pp. 66-67)

Did you catch that? According to deep ecology, your "self" does not stop at the outer limits of your skin. You become a whole person, a spiritually mature person, only by the realization of "'self-in-Self' where 'Self' stands for organic wholeness." The capital-S *Self* includes "not only me, an individual human, but all humans, whales, grizzly bears, whole rain forest ecosystems, mountains and rivers, the tiniest microbes in the soil, and so on." How do you arrive at such a state of expanded Self? By a "meditative deep questioning process" (ibid., 67).

Biocentric equality. Deep ecology's second "ultimate norm" is biocentric equality. The phrase means that "all things in the biosphere have an equal right to live and blossom and . . . are _equal in intrinsic worth_" (ibid., 67, emphasis added).

Here deep ecology acknowledges a problem by claiming that all things have equal worth and an equal right to live and flourish. In the real world, animals do not recognize such a right; they kill and eat each other. Even vegetarians kill and eat plants to keep themselves alive.

Human beings do not eat rocks, and we have no stomach for eating only those things that have died of themselves. We cannot live without killing something. Deep ecology tries to get around this difficulty by saying that we have the right to take life in order to satisfy our _vital_ needs.

What needs are "vital" and who decides? Deep ecologists admit that human beings' _vital_ needs go beyond food, water, and shelter to include love, play, creative expression, intimate relationships with nature and other humans, and spiritual growth. Killing to satisfy those needs therefore would be acceptable by deep ecology's rules (ibid., 68).

Sources of knowledge. Deep ecology's "two ultimate norms" have implications far beyond recycling cans or eating less meat. Where did they come from? They are "arrived at by the deep questioning process and reveal the importance of moving to the philosophical and religious level of wisdom. They cannot be validated, of course, by the methodology of modern science based on its usual mechanistic assumptions and its very narrow definition of data" (ibid., 66).

Of course that is an anathema to the technological viewpoint of the environment, which holds that scientific research is the way to find truth. In and of itself that doesn't prove deep ecology is anathema to Christians. We fully agree that there are norms for human life that cannot be validated by science. We agree that there is an intuitive side of life by which we sometimes reach valid conclusions.

God speaks to people in ways that are not measurable or explainable by science. God at times reveals to human beings his expectations, his character, and what he is going to do. He even revealed himself in a man, Jesus Christ, superseding some (though not all) natural laws in order to do it. If all knowledge and wisdom could be arrived at scientifically, we would be back at the Enlightenment from which so many of our problems came.

There are, however, severe difficulties with deep ecology, just as there are difficulties with the technological viewpoint. But before we get into a Christian answer to either of those views and before we try to begin building a uniquely Christian ecology, we need to examine a claim frequently made by environmentalists on both sides: that Christian belief is actually responsible for earth's ecological problems.

CHAPTER FOUR
IS CHRISTIANITY TO BLAME?

We who defend Christianity find ourselves
constantly opposed not by the irreligion of our hearers
but by their real religion.
C.S. Lewis, Miracles

S ince you're reading this book, you're most likely a Christian concerned about the state of this earth. Your faith in God has led you to become interested in caring for his creation.

In that case it has probably surprised you to learn that in the popular secular view of ecology, you and your belief system are the cause of the problem.

Read very much secular environmental writing and you find that historic biblical Christianity gets a very bad press.

The patriarchal, aloof, authoritarian, separatist Christian God is the cause of our ecological sickness, we're told. We must get back into harmony with the earthy, primitive life-force that inhabits all things, the matriarchal womb of the earth our Mother, and recognize our oneness with Divinity. The aboriginal peoples knew this before Western imperialism destroyed them; those remaining keep it alive despite Christian missionaries who try to impose their culture.

Where did these accusations come from? More importantly, are they true?

An Important Accusation

The attack on Christianity as the cause of environmental degradation is usually traced to a 1967 article in *Science* magazine by Lynn White, Jr., titled "The Historical Roots of Our Ecologic Crisis."

Dr. White was not an ecologist but a professor of Medieval and Renaissance history who had published several books on the development of Western culture. White's article came at a propitious place and time, appearing in a popular magazine just when the foundational values of American culture were being severely questioned by a well-educated younger generation—questioned not only in the towers of universities but publicly in the streets.

White said that the root of the ecological problem lies in the combining of technology and science "as a normal pattern of action," a union that revolutionized society toward the middle of the nineteenth century. It was the culmination of a centuries-long European leadership in both technology (water power, wind power, glass-making, ship-building, the mechanical clock) and in science (leadership passed to Europe from Islamic scientists in the late thirteenth century). Since the European science and technology we have inherited developed in the Middle Ages, he asks what the fundamental medieval assumptions were. By looking at history we can discover "the presuppositions that underlie modern technology and science." (You'll recall that is what we did in Chapter 2, but White came up with different results.)

So-called "Christian axioms"

The heart of White's thesis is his statement, "We continue today to live, as we have lived for about 1700 years, very largely in a context of Christian axioms." He then shows that those supposed axioms are devastating to the natural environment: "Our daily habits of action . . .

are dominated by an implicit faith in perpetual progress which was unknown either to Greco-Roman antiquity or to the Orient. It is rooted in, and is indefensible apart from, Judeo-Christian teleology."

Teleology is a good theological word from the Greek *telos* or *end*. It has to do with purpose, maturity, perfection, and completeness. It is the "completion" that God will accomplish in our lives at the day of Christ (Phil. 1:6). White says that because Christians perceive human history not as circular but as going somewhere—which is accurate— we have a faith in progress that other cultures do not share.

Because those of us steeped in Christian teaching see ourselves as made in God's image, "Christianity is the most anthropocentric religion the world has seen. . . . Christianity, in absolute contrast to ancient paganism and Asia's religions (except, perhaps, Zoroastrianism), not only established a dualism of man and nature but also insisted that it is God's will that man exploit nature for his proper ends."

Primitive cultures had their animistic guardian spirits in the mountains, trees, and brooks. These had to be placated before a man could mine the mountain, cut down the tree, dam the brook. Christianity was indifferent to these spirits and so could harvest the resources freely.

An inconsistent case

If basic Christian teachings are at the root of the exploitation of nature, why has Eastern Christianity not shown significant technological advances? Interestingly, White acknowledges this discrepancy:

> What I have said may well apply to the medieval West, where in fact technology made spectacular advances. But the Greek East, a highly civilized realm of equal Christian devotion, seems to have produced no marked technological innovation after the late 7th Century. (White, "The Historical Roots of Our Ecologic Crisis," *Science*)

45

He attributed this phenomenon to "a difference in the tonality of piety and thought"; but if Christian theology produces exploitative technology, we would expect to find its effects in *all* places "of equal Christian devotion." What White failed to acknowledge is that the Eastern Church was unaffected by the European Enlightenment where, as we saw in Chapter 2, nature was cut off from God and faith in progress arose.

Abuse Is Universal

Even Lynn White had to admit that ecological devastation is not unique to Western "Christian" cultures. He referred to the lower Nile in pre-Christian times as "a human artifact rather than the swampy African jungle which nature, apart from man, would have made it." He also wrote about "the cutting of forest [in North Africa] by the Romans to build ships" that profoundly altered the ecology of that area.

In the 1950s China was often cited as an example of what happens when a country fails to protect its soil from erosion.

Chinese geographer Yi-Fu Tuan confirms:

Visitors to China in the nineteenth and early part of the twentieth centuries have often commented on the treelessness of the North, and the acute problems of soil erosion on the loess-covered plateaus. These areas were once well wooded. Deforestation on a vast scale took place as population increased and more and more land was taken over by farmers. But this alone does not account for the extent of the clearing. Other factors militated against prudence. One was the ancient custom, first recorded in the fourth century B.C., of burning trees in order to deprive dangerous animals of their hiding places. Even in contemporary China farmers are known to start fires for no evident purpose.

Forests in North China were also depleted to make charcoal for industrial fuel. From the tenth century on, the expanding metallic industries swallowed up many hundreds of thousands of tons of charcoal each year, as did the manufacture of salt, alum, bricks, tile, and liquor. By the Sung dynasty (960-1279 A.D.) the demand for wood and charcoal as both household and industrial fuels had exceeded the timber resources of the country; the result was the increasing substitution of coal for wood and charcoal. (Tuan, "Our Treatment of the Environment in Ideal and Actuality," *American Scientist*)

Tuan also wrote that "Lines in Sophocles' *Antigone* refer to the power of man to tear the soil with his plow. Plato in *Critias* described the negative side of that power—deforestation and soil erosion." He continued:

But the Romans did far more than the Greeks to impose their will on the natural environment. "Public roads," as Gibbons wrote in admiration, "ran in a direct line from one city to another, with very little respect for the obstacles of either nature or of private property. Mountains were perforated, and bold arches thrown over the broadest and most rapid streams." (Ibid., 247)

Closer to home, the native American respect for "brother beaver" paled in the light of the white man's trinkets, knives, and blankets. The Hudson Bay Company and the Northwest Company set up trading posts across the continent to trade with the Indians for the valued pelts to make fashionable beaver hats. During the seventeenth and eighteenth centuries an army of *voyageurs* was needed to transport goods west for trade with the Indians and carry the beaver pelts back to the east coast for shipment to Europe. While whites provided the market, in the early days it was the Indians who willingly provided the pelts.

The evidence of these and other examples is that the history of disrespect for nature is much broader than Western culture with its Judeo-Christian heritage. While we can agree with Lynn White that "the roots of our trouble are largely religious," we find no historical foundation for singling out the Christian religion for promoting an exploitative view of nature.

Hebrews and the earth

It's notable that in his 1967 article White concentrated on the Christian religion and avoided the issue of Hebrew religion, though both have equal roots in Genesis.

The mandate to have dominion over the earth dates from the first page of the Old Testament; it was Hebrew for thousands of years before it was Christian. If belief in God-given dominion over nature gives license to exploit the earth, history should reveal a Hebrew society bursting with invention and busy getting the most out of this creation God gave them.

That is exactly what we do *not* find in archaeology or the Bible. The Israelites were never known as technological wizards. Their food and drink during the Exodus journey was credited to miraculous manna and quail and water from the rock, not to their cleverness at exploiting the desert. Aaron did have the technical skill to fashion a golden calf-god, but his work is not a bright spot in Jewish history (Exod. 32:2-4).

When the Israelites first entered Canaan, they were stymied by the people of the plains who had chariots of iron (Judg. 1:19). Their eventual conquest of Canaan was due to God's intervention rather than superior weapons. The wonderful construction of Moses' tabernacle and Solomon's temple were attributed to plans dictated directly by God rather than architectural brilliance. Huram (or Hiram) the metal-working expert, half-Jew and half-Gentile, had to be brought to Jerusalem from Tyre in order to make the utensils for the temple (1 Kings 7:13-14). In health matters the Hebrews were ahead of their time in diet and cleanliness, but those habits were credited to revealed laws of conduct rather than medical research and development. Hezekiah's water-tunnel at Jerusalem (2 Kings 20:20) stands out because it is such an unusual technical accomplishment.

History looks back to the Romans for their public works projects and the Greeks for their scientific inquiries, but it does not look back to the Hebrews for any technological brilliance.

The God of True Christianity

If the separation of God from nature began with the biblical creation story, the result ought to be a human-centered Bible with God as a distant figure. Again this is exactly what we do not find. In the Bible not every rock is claimed to be inhabited by God, but neither is God ever very far away from his world. Biblical people spend more time running from God—or meeting up with him in unexpected places—than they spend searching for him because he is "up there" and they can't find him.

"Surely the LORD is in this place, and I was not aware of it," Jacob marveled in the middle of nowhere at Bethel. "How awesome is this place! This is none other than the house of God; this is the gate of heaven" (Gen. 28:16-17).

The psalmist wrote:

Where can I go from your Spirit?
  Where can I flee from your presence?
If I go up to the heavens, you are there;
  if I make my bed in the depths, you are there.
If I rise on the wings of the dawn,
  if I settle on the far side of the sea,
even there your hand will guide me,
  your right hand will hold me fast. (Ps. 139:7-10)

God with us, not aloof

Perhaps then the fault is with the reinterpretation of the Old Testament by the New; Christian doctrine must be to blame for distancing God from nature. But does the accusation fit the facts? It certainly does not fit a faith that rests on *Incarnation:* God walking on this earth in physical flesh.

49

Christianity claims a God who *could* have stayed aloof but becomes *involved* in this world, a Savior "by whom all things were made; who for us men, and for our salvation, came down from heaven; and was incarnate by the Holy Ghost of the Virgin Mary, and was made man; and was crucified also for us under Pontius Pilate. He suffered and was buried; and the third day he rose again according to the Scriptures" (from the Nicene Creed).

In Christian faith, God is the very *opposite* of a distant figure uninvolved with the planet. He is intimately involved with this earth in the ultimate way: He becomes a creature like us. He walks the dusty roads, grows tired, becomes thirsty, gets irritated, grieves over the squabbling and the betrayals and the deaths of his friends. As he passes through the countryside he is a close observer of nature; we know that by the natural imagery in his teachings. Soil, seeds, fish, sheep, goats, birds, flowers, trees, the sky, light, water—all figure into his teaching. "The parables of Jesus lifted a veil from the face of Nature; they connect the things of sense to the things of faith" (Wood, "The Intimacy of Jesus with Nature," *London Quarterly & Holborn Review).* And he even experiences nature *in extremis*—he goes through what no god should have to go through, physical death.

The Incarnation is a deeper involvement, a far more profound commitment, than any god could make who is already "part of earth." God is Spirit who *by choice* "became flesh and made his dwelling among us" (John 1:14). He humbled himself from Godhood to manhood (Phil. 2:6-8).

He also promised his disciples "I will not leave you as orphans; I will come to you" when he pledged the Holy Spirit "to be with you forever" (John 14:16, 18).

Christianity says that God has made an eternal commitment of intimacy with this world.

Early Christian evidence

That is good theory, but what about the practice of the early Christians? Is there evidence that they got busy exploiting the earth with their incarnate Savior's blessing? The facts point the other direction. They refused to buy into the power structures of the cultures around them.

In the early 1950s, French sociologist and Catholic layman Jacques Ellul wrote a remarkable critique of the mechanization of culture, titled *La Technique,* translated in the 1960s to *The Technological Society.* Years before the popular environmental movement pointed the finger of ecological blame at Christianity, Ellul wrote this:

> It is not a coincidence that Rome declined as Christianity triumphed. The Emperor Julian was certainly justified in accusing the Christians of ruining the industry of the Empire.
>
> After this period of decadence (for which, of course, Christianity was not solely responsible), what does the historian find? The restoration, under Christian influence, of an active civilization—methodical, exploiting the riches of the world as a gift given by God to be put to good use? Not at all. The society that developed from the tenth to the fourteenth century was vital, coherent, and unanimous; but it was characterized by a total absence of the technological will. It was "a-capitalistic" as well as "a-technical." . . . Only architectural technique developed and asserted itself; but this was prompted not by a technical state of mind but by religious impulse. . . .
>
> And when at the beginning of the twelfth century, at first very feebly a technical movement began to take form, it developed under the influence of the East. (Ellul, *The Technological Society,* p. 34)

You still see a similar instinct in modern intentional Christian communities or in any group that attempts to get back to the way things were done by the early Christians. Their move is nearly always in the direction of simplicity rather than away from it. They reduce their standard of living by retreating to simplified rural life, or, if they live in the city, they share cars and other resources. Think of the Amish and Bruderhof communities. They are marked by less drive for material wealth, not more. Of course that may be because they are trying to "get back" in history to New Testament times. But if there is a drive for dominion inherent in basic Christianity, why do these most basic Christians not display it?

We often see the same phenomenon when a materially successful person becomes a Christian. Gadgets and status symbols suddenly become less important and are often disposed of. The person's urge is often to get back to the heart of life, the basics.

Many people look back affectionately to their time at a Christian camp as their doorway to a deeper spiritual life. What is the philosophy of Christian camping? To get young people out into the natural world so they can better encounter God. Appreciating nature and meeting God are so obviously entwined that anyone involved with Christian camping must be surprised to hear Christians accused of abusing nature.

Empty Accusations

So it is a mistake to blame earth's problems on the concept of dominion under God. As we saw in Chapter 2, it was when God was taken *out* of nature that the roots of the earth's devastation were set free to grow. Enlightenment thinkers saw science as a way of making nature more useful as humanity gained mastery over nature. Both Adam Smith and John Stuart Mill portrayed nature as merely the raw materials for human industry and economy. Rather than Christians "chopping down sacred groves," as White would have us believe, it was the leaders of the Enlightenment who pushed God out of the picture, leaving nature unprotected in a world gone secular.

Looking at history, then, we find that it is inappropriate to hold the Bible responsible for modern humanity's dramatically changed relationship to nature. . . .

We need to look elsewhere to discover the roots of modern

humanity's relationship to nature. The answer, in my judgment, is found largely in understanding the impact of the Enlightenment and the scientific revolution on how we all think about, and relate to, nature. The secularization of nature has its roots not in the Bible, but in the evolution of modern thinking, according to which humanity removed itself from nature in order to objectively observe, understand, and ultimately control it. (Granberg-Michaelson, *A Worldly Spirituality,* p. 41)

Lynn White's thesis had early Christian critics. Zoologist Wilbur L. Bullock, for example, allowed that there was some truth in White's charge, but added:

The most serious weakness I see in White's position is that it lumps too much into the one pot of "orthodox Christianity." He fails to recognize that probably the greatest exploitation was done by people who had only the vaguest, most perfunctory association with any form of Christianity. Furthermore, these exploiters were interested in their own selfish gain, a motive distinctly contrary to the self-denial of true Christian love. (Bullock, "The Coming Catastrophes: Causes and Remedies," *Journal of the American Scientific Association*)

In 1970 (in the same magazine that had given White a forum) Lewis W. Moncrief challenged White's thesis—and the growing acceptance of it by theologians—saying, "I would suggest that the wide acceptance of such a simplistic explanation is at this point based more on fad than on fact." (Unfortunately the "fad" has continued for a quarter of a century.) Moncrief asked whether the finger could not be pointed at *all* cultures:

No culture has been able to completely screen out the egocentric tendencies of human beings. . . . If non-Judeo-Christian cultures had the same levels of economic productivity, urbanization, and high average household incomes, is there evidence to indicate that these cultures would not exploit or disregard nature as our culture does? If our environmental crisis is a "religious problem," why are other parts of the world experiencing in various degrees the same environmental problems that we are so well acquainted with in the Western world? (Moncrief, "The Cultural Basis for Our Environmental Crisis," *Science)*

In the past quarter-century the attack on Christianity has grown rather than lessened. It has come out of the intellectual fringe and entered the mainstream. There is an increasingly overt demand for doing away with its outmoded exclusivist thought patterns in favor of a worldwide consensus of right thinking.

When the evidence is so strong that many cultures with many religions are guilty of abusing the earth, why is Christianity still picked on? Father Vincent Rossi offers a possible explanation:

It was only when western civilization "liberated" itself from Christianity and its traditional doctrinal restraints that the door was opened for the ecological disasters of the present day. A truly impartial reading of history makes this fact so clear that one wonders at the persistent and pervasive hostility so many environmentalists display toward Christianity. . . . One would almost think that many people want to use Christianity as a convenient scapegoat. (Rossi, "Theocentrism: The Cornerstone of Christian Ecology," *Epiphany Journal)*

Christianity as a faith cannot be held responsible for an exploitative attitude toward earth. Once our belief system is excused of blame, we may be tempted to wash our hands of earth's problems and feel righteous that we have not really done any damage. But the matter is not so simple as that. Regardless of who is "to blame," we have to look honestly at how Christians *have* responded to the reality of God's damaged earth.

CHAPTER FIVE
A RAGGED CHRISTIAN RESPONSE

The year's at the spring
And day's at the morn;
Morning's at seven;
The hill-side's dew-pearled;
The lark's on the wing;
The snail's on the thorn:
God's in his heaven—
All's right with the world!
Robert Browning, "Pippa Passes"

U sually at Christmas we receive an assortment of religious cards (Mary and Joseph, Jesus in the manger, the star, wise men, etc.) and secular cards (Santa, reindeer, sleds, stockings hung from mantles, and so forth). This year there's something different. This Christmas, we are getting Nature cards. In our card display taped along the woodwork, the familiar red and green give way to earth-tones of wolves, whitetail deer, and trees (not cut Christmas trees). The verses inside wish us all the joys the natural world has to offer at this season and in the New Year.

We have gotten used to Santa displacing Jesus. Is Nature now displacing Santa?

Celebrating Suzy Snowflake?

Bah humbug? Please don't misunderstand. (And if we're on your Christmas card list, please don't take us off.) We're glad that "nature" Christmas cards are printed on recycled paper and that earth tones mean less bleach and less dye. Yet don't we detect a cultural trend?

Is this Christmastime celebration of nature only an extension of the celebration of the Incarnation, by which God entered nature and shared our earthly flesh? Or are we right to detect a new faith nudging itself into both the religious and the secular observance of the holiday?

Columnist Dave Barry was pretty sure which way to interpret the trend when he observed that the traditional school "Christmas" concert had turned into a celebration of "weather":

At my son's school, they now hold the winter program in February and sing increasingly nonmemorable songs such as "Winter Wonderland," "Frosty the Snowman" and—this is a real song—"Suzy Snowflake." . . . A visitor from another planet would assume that the children belonged to the Church of Meteorology. (Barry, "Notes on Western Civilization," *Chicago Tribune Magazine)*

No one knows for sure in which season of the year Christ was born. Christmas was placed into December to counter the pagan Roman holiday of Saturnalia. Now, it seems, we're finally seeing the Pagans' Revenge: the usurping process is being reversed. Around here some people dance around fires to celebrate the December 21 winter solstice (and the summer solstice and the spring and fall equinoxes as well). They are the ones who honestly confess their conversion to pagan nature religion.

Others who love the natural world are not so eager to deny their Christian roots. They would just like to see the natural world get more attention from the church, and Christmas seems a logical time to do it.

Growing earth-awareness in the church

No matter how you interpret it, Christian religious expression is sounding more earth-centered. In the past twenty years earth-aware language has been written into creeds and hymns and Bible schools and educational curriculum everywhere.

In some Christian traditions, of course, faith has long been "earth-centered" in the sense that this world is affirmed as the gritty arena where humankind works, suffers, rejoices, and meets God. What we're talking about is something different. The new expression of Christianity is "earth-centered" in the sense that its vision of spirituality is wrapped up in knowing and honoring *the natural earth itself.*

The revised creeds and environmental-awareness curricula prove that the accusations of Lynn White and his colleagues have not gone unanswered. Christian theological publications on the creation and humanity's role in caring for creation shot skyward in the late 60s and early 70s, with a giant jump in 1970.

FIGURE 1. Publications relating the Judeo-Christian tradition and the Creation (1950-1988).

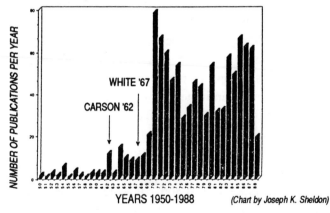

YEARS 1950-1988 *(Chart by Joseph K. Sheldon)*

The papers, articles, and books have not all been in defense of Christianity. Many have been *mea culpa* apologizing and taking the blame for the way we Western Christians have divorced ourselves from the earth, exploited its resources, and destroyed primitive societies that could have taught us about living in harmony with the

57

natural world. We've already made our case that blaming Christianity for the ecological problem is unfair, but that does not mean all Christians are innocent of damaging the earth. To say that the Enlightenment separated nature from God and gave humanity the idea that nature existed to be exploited is not to excuse Christians from any share of responsibility for the exploitation.

Christianity and Culture

In the first place, the Christian faith flourishes in this world and inevitably adopts some of the values of the culture in which it is planted. We can't help it; we live here, and we're human.

The church's earliest conflicts were cultural clashes. From New Testament times, for example, there were debates over just how "Jewish" Gentile converts needed to become, as well as which Gentile customs were inappropriate to their new faith. Read Acts 15, the book of Galatians, Romans 14, 1 Corinthians 8 and 10, and you see Christians trying to come to terms with their own (and each other's) cultural loyalties.

As the church found acceptance within the Roman Empire, it began to adapt Roman festivals and holidays to Christian celebrations, giving us many of our Easter and Christmas traditions. The early Enlightenment thinkers started out as part of the church, so their thinking had its effects within the church as well as outside.

Today the church still adapts to the surrounding culture, but it's harder for us to see, living as we do within both church and culture. It's nearly impossible to sort out which of our values are derived from our faith and which have come from growing up in a particular society.

In American history, the value that has permeated both culture and church and that has greatest implications for ecology is the idea of "progress."

Faith in progress

From the beginning of the history of the U.S., there was an unquenchable faith in humanity's ability to overcome natural obstacles and prosper in the making, buying, and selling of this world's goods.

> The idea of progress was given a prominent place in both secular and religious thinking. The typical thinker of the Enlightenment was optimistic about man and confident that his destiny on earth would involve a continual conquest of nature and ever greater human felicity. In Christian terms, this would lead to a postmillennial eschatology; that is, the kingdom of God would be realized in history, whereupon Christ or his Spirit would in some sense return. (Ahlstrom, *A Religious History of the American People,* p. 357)

There was a continual shift from the Puritan ideal of spiritual progress to a material/economic vision of progress. John Winthrop, first governor of the Massachusetts Bay Colony, expressed his dream of the Puritan community as a model for the world to follow, an image cherished by Ronald Reagan: "We shall find that the God of Israel is among us. . . . For we must consider that we shall be a city upon a hill, the eyes of all the people are upon us" (Miller, *The American Puritans*, p. 83).

Even Jonathan Edwards, known best for his role in the "Great Awakening," was influenced by the Enlightenment philosophers John Locke and Isaac Newton simply because of the times he lived in (see Garrett, "Jonathan Edwards and the Great Awakening," *American Christianity: A Case Approach,* p. 23).

In the nineteenth century Americans moved westward, and the church followed with emotional revivals on the frontier. It was "a movement deeply rooted in the Puritan's compulsion to transform the world, the democratic American's conviction that men ought to be free, and the new Adam's soaring faith in human progress" (Ahlstrom, *A Religious History,* p. 427). By the end of the nineteenth century a Social Gospel message was the major theme of the "liberal" church. Walter Rauschenbusch's *Christianity and the Social Crisis* expresses the optimism of its spirit:

> The swiftness of evolution in our own country proves the immense latent perfectibility in human nature. . . . If at this juncture we can rally sufficient religious faith and moral strength to snap the bonds of evil and turn the present unparalleled economic and intellectual resources of humanity to the harmonious development of a true social life, the generations yet unborn will mark this as that great day of the Lord for which ages have waited, and count us blessed for sharing in the apostolate that proclaimed it. (Rauschenbusch, *Christianity and the Social Crisis,* p. 422)

Whose view of progress?

American Christians shared the idea of inevitable progress, but they came into conflict over the spiritual versus the material/economic visions of progress. Among the Puritans the conflict was between poor and wealthy, often over questions of land inheritance. Later it was the question of whether slavery could be justified in a "free society." Temporarily, profit took precedence over moral considerations in the rising industrialism of the nineteenth century.

In both slavery and industrialization, the various denominations took a stand on various sides of the issues. There was certainly no unified Christian stand against slavery. Ahlstrom writes that on the road to the Civil War, in the hardening of attitudes both for and against slavery, "the churches were a powerful factor. They provided the traditional recourse and appeal to the Absolute. They gave moral grandeur to the antislavery cause and divine justification for slavery" (Ahlstrom, *A Religious History,* p. 668). Churches such as the Methodists and Baptists split over the issue of slavery.

Despite the "Social Gospel," as urbanization and industrialization grew the church was slow to stand up against the terrible conditions of the nineteenth-century immigrant factory worker. "Much of

Protestantism, especially that of a far earlier immigration, defended the position of the business community" (Gaustad, *A Religious History of America,* p. 242).

A favorite theme of evangelist D.L. Moody was the mother at home praying for the souls of her husband and sons who had gone out into the temptations of the world. The perceived foundation of spiritual life had shifted—from a "city on a hill" where holy people worked to create a holy society, to "home and mother" where the workplace was outside the spiritual realm.

A loss of distinctives

It is interesting to note certain churches that began among the poor and working classes but have now shed their "poverty" images. They are no longer the little church with peeling paint on the wrong side of the tracks; their sleek new buildings have every modern convenience. They have had to change because their congregations have become embarrassingly affluent. Some have even revised their message to proclaim a "health and wealth gospel."

In the United States, Christianity as a religion has absorbed so much of the culture that descended from the Enlightenment that much of what is labeled "Christian" is only a shadow of its New Testament source. The church has shed its distinctives as the community of people who have been transformed by the personal Redeemer.

It's not surprising, then, that the church has had little to say about ecology that is distinctively Christian, just as it often has trouble making distinctively Christian commentary on any social problem.

Some Christian Responses

To the credit of many modern churches, there have been sincere attempts to respond to the ecological crisis both theologically and practically. The movement is mostly in the "mainline" denominations. Some are trying hard to educate and motivate their memberships to be more aware of earth's needs and to take seriously our responsibilities under God.

Often, however, we find that as churches have published their environmental materials, they have (wittingly or unwittingly) bought into secular environmentalists' mistrust of Christianity and incorporated supposed native American and East Asian spiritual ideas: the land being "sacred," a blurring of the distinctions between ourselves and other forms of life, and recognition of the earth as a personified Mother who gave us life. The publications are often emotionally compelling and have good advice about land stewardship, but they do not present a *Christian* response in any sense except that they were published by a church.

Sometimes the confusion is apparently unintended. The educational materials were obviously put together eclectically by people who were not critical thinkers.

Other times, however, the syncretistic approach clearly springs from ideals of "tolerance" and "pluralism" rather than from confidence in the uniqueness of biblical revelation. The writers clearly (and rightly) believe that a spiritual solution is needed. But they do not believe Christianity has anything *uniquely* good to offer in the area of ecology, so they assemble a mixture of "spiritual" approaches.

The result betrays the fact that the writers' approach is in fact neither tolerant nor pluralistic. It usually winds up promoting the primitive earth-centered religions that supposedly have it all over Christianity in *true* spirituality, which is taken to equal honoring of the sacredness of the land.

Emergency solutions

Besides a basic mistrust of historical biblical Christianity, there is a mood of nervous urgency, a faithlessness, about some of the environmental materials published by churches. God's sustaining care for his creation gets overlooked. The assumption is that it's entirely up to *us* to save the earth, and we must save it or else. This urgency begs for the emergency construction of a new brand of faith to rescue us from disaster.

Ron Sider reports a call for a religious effort on behalf of ecology—from a surprising source:

> In the opening words of his famous book and TV series, *Cosmos,* [Carl] Sagan solemnly affirms the nonexistence of God: "Cosmos is all that is or ever was or ever will be." But our situation is so desperate, Sagan believes, that the support of religious leaders is nonetheless essential if we are to avoid environmental disaster. . . .
>
> More than a year ago an international circle of prestigious scientists led by Sagan had issued an urgent appeal to religious leaders, confessing that only the full support of religious conviction could avert environmental disaster. Many religious leaders responded favorably and called for joint action. The result was a meeting of religious leaders in New York in June, 1991. Happily, Evangelicals for Social Action took hold of the opportunity to have a voice in the development of the program and to select evangelical church leaders to participate. Future meetings like it are expected. (Sider, "Green Theology," *ESA Advocate)*

It's important for evangelicals to have a voice in gatherings like the one in New York, because once people abandon the authority of Scripture and the unique revelation of Jesus Christ, the next step is to embrace whatever form of religion promises to meet the need of the moment. It is a perfectly logical step. If the earth has an urgent problem and if the old religion hasn't solved it (maybe has even caused it) then it is necessary to find some religion that *will* solve the problem before it's too late.

A prediction come true

A 1954 article by Joseph Sittler, Jr., then of Chicago Lutheran Theological Seminary, was prophetic. Professor Sittler's concern was not so much ecology as the church's growing separation of the gospel from earthly life, but his words have come true in the area of ecology.

> When orthodox Christianity refuses to articulate a theology for the earth, the clamant hurt of God's ancient creation is not thereby silenced. Earth's voices, the collective of her lost grace and her destined redemption, will speak through one or another form of naturalism. If the Church will not have a theology *for* nature, then irresponsible but sensitive men will act as midwives for nature's unsilenceable meaningfulness, and enunciate a theology of nature. (Sittler, "A Theology for Earth," *The Christian Scholar)*

That is exactly what has happened. The church has been slow to respond to the issue of ecology, and meanwhile people who do not acknowledge the God of biblical revelation but who care deeply about nature have moved into the vacuum and articulated a "theology of nature." Christianity does not strike them as a persuasive and attractive option. They exclude it from their thinking and go on to other faiths, or construct their own eclectic religion custom-made to fit the ecological gap.

A Fox for our time
A most interesting religious approach to ecology is the rise of "creation spirituality." Its revered elder statesman is Matthew Fox, and all Christians who talk with spiritually oriented environmentalists should be familiar with him.

Fox is a Dominican priest gifted with a persuasive and seductive use of words (as well as a memorable name and physical appearance). For a time he was silenced by the church for his views. In the last interview he granted before his enforced period of silence, he talked with Sam Keen (a disciple of mythologist Joseph Campbell) about "creation spirituality," which he calls "liberation theology for the First World, for the overdeveloped peoples." Fox calls his view *panentheism,* "which says the image of God or divinity is immanent in all things but that God transcends the created order." Practically speaking, however, his view equals pantheism (the belief that all is God).

When Keen asked him the very important question, "What part does Christ play in your scheme of things?" Fox replied:

> Fundamentalists and liberal theologians have one thing in common. I call it Jesus-olatry. They concentrate so much on Jesus that they miss the cosmic Christ and the divinity within creation. And, what is even stranger, they even miss the message of the gospels. . . .
>
>   The Gospel of John begins with the assertion that Christ is the Word, the Logos, the indwelling divine reason within things. The cosmic Christ is in the soil, in the rain forest, in the body and in the pain of the world. . . . Far from underplaying the part of Jesus, I frankly think *we're recovering the cosmic Christ that was at the center of the New Testament tradition.* (Keen, "Original Blessing, Not Original Sin," *Psychology Today,* emphasis added)

Matthew Fox claims to have unearthed the true roots of Christian faith, but he has actually rewritten Christianity to fit the new spirituality he believes is demanded by our age. He is one "having a form of godliness but denying its power" (2 Tim. 3:5).

> I have been arguing that the new symbol of Jesus as Mother Earth crucified yet rising holds power to awaken humans to the survival of Mother Earth, to the elimination of matricide, and to their own best selves as mystics, prophets, and creative persons. . . . The bottom line is not that Christianity survive into the next millennium. . . . Nothing will survive if Mother Earth does not survive. The issue is the survival, and indeed the thriving, of Mother Earth. (Fox, *The Coming of the Cosmic Christ,* p. 149)

Here we find Christianity evolved into a wholly other religion. Ethics becomes a matter not of obedience but of *survival*. The person of the historical Jesus is belittled; Christ becomes Mother Earth, crucified and rising again. As Christians we find our true identity in "the Cosmic Christ . . . the 'I am' in every creature" (Fox, *Cosmic Christ,* p. 154). Fox believes that we should turn away from our warped focus on original sin and replace it with the idea of "original blessing"—God has pronounced all things good and we must look upon them as good, not fallen.

"Creation spirituality" confuses the issue of the church's response to ecology. Though when held against the Bible it is not a genuinely Christian response, it is being articulated by representatives of churches (both Catholic and Protestant) and therefore is *identified* as a Christian response.

It is a *new* faith rather than a revised Christianity that the Irish Catholic missionary Sean McDonagh seeks when he writes:

> There is much that Christians can learn from the approach of tribal religions which might prevent us abusing the natural world. Tribal people are sensitive to spirit presence in the world around them.

What is McDonagh looking for when he seeks environmental answers among the people of "tribal religions"?

> A new spirituality which sees the Earth as permeated with the divine presence would undoubtedly provide the basis for world-wide co-operation among religious people today to respect and care for the Earth. (McDonagh, *To Care for the Earth: A Call to a New Theology,* pp. 109-110, 152)

The idea of looking at other religions for helpful concepts can be good if done critically, but disastrous if done with the idea that in other religions we might find something more enlightened, more true, closer to God than "the faith that was once for all entrusted to the saints" (Jude 3).

Another view: there's no problem

At the other end of the Christian spectrum, some take a more direct approach to the dominion command. In the book we quoted in Chapter 3, E. Calvin Beisner is blunt about his perceived purpose of the earth and our place on it:

> While it may be ambiguous about other things, the dominion mandate clearly means that the earth, with everything in it—though it all belongs to God (Ps. 24:1)—was intended by God to serve man's needs. Man was not made for the earth; the earth was made for man. It is man, not the earth or anything in it, who was created in the image of God. To make man subservient to the earth is to turn the purpose of God in creation on its head. . . . Within the limits of God's moral Law, any use of resources that serves people is permissible; the more efficiently it serves them, the better it is. . . . Freedom, not constraint, must be the rule here. (Beisner, *Prospects For Growth,* pp. 163, 168)

Other Christians agree to the point of denying that the earth is really running out of resources. Lindsey Williams, who ministered as chaplain to workers on the Trans-Alaska Oil Pipeline, claims he discovered that the U.S. government is concealing the world's richest oil deposits off the north slope of Alaska. "There is no true energy crisis," he wrote in 1980. "There never has been an energy crisis . . . except as it has been produced by the Federal government for the purpose of controlling the American people" (Williams, *The Energy Non-Crisis,* p. 13).

"Green Christianity"

Still another, very different Christian perspective is found in Tim Cooper's book *Green Christianity,* published in England. Cooper, a member of the Green party in England, seeks to bring his Christian faith into the Greens' concern for the environment. He sees hope because

> A new, Green economics is slowly emerging which embraces many Old Testament principles concerning economic life, such as the need to restrain the accumulation of wealth, to achieve justice through a "bias to the poor" in public policy, and to focus upon stewardship rather than ownership. . . . A Christian society should be measured not by the size of its gross national product, but by the quality of people's relationships with the Creator and with each other. (Cooper, *Green Christianity,* p. 101)

There are dangers in Christians aligning themselves closely with the Green movement, a danger Cooper recognizes: "The starting point of Green thinking is not *necessarily* Christ but observation of our surroundings; it is biocentric, not Christocentric." Because the Greens recognize the spiritual nature of the problems of ecology, Cooper recognizes the danger of going along with the faith on which they base their ideals: "A fundamental allegiance to the Earth and its evolution, however, implies an inclination towards paganism, a faith in the Earth as a self-regulating entity." But because he shares much of the Greens' vision of how the world should be, Cooper is happy to go along with much of the Green movement and feels it is consistent with his Christian faith (ibid., 109-110).

Reasons for Rejection

Whenever people adapt or invent religions they are, of course, expressing their free will. Even when Christianity is presented thoughtfully and persuasively, some people choose to be turned off. There are at least three reasons many sincere environmentalists reject or at least try to discredit Christianity.

First, as we've seen, there has been silence or waffling about the problem on the part of Christians.

Second, they see more hope in the religions of primitive non-Christian cultures that pay great attention to supposed spiritual forces in the earth. Christian missionaries are accused of putting the damper on these religions, and it's true that missionaries encourage converts to reject animism—not from disregard for ecology but because they no longer have anything to fear from the earth gods.

Third, they know enough about Christianity to know that it encompasses larger issues and makes deeper claims on us than *just* how we treat the earth. Personal morality, the admission that we are sinners, the need for salvation, the call to holiness—all are inherent in Christianity and all are an affront to raw human nature.

So we can understand why environmental activists construct their own eclectic religions to meet the ecological challenge. When such eclectic religions continue to use Christian *language,* they muddy the waters of the Christian response to ecology.

Signs of Evangelical Interest

All the mainline Protestant denominations and the Catholic Church have made efforts to respond to the ecology crisis. There is particularly encouraging response among evangelicals. The Au Sable Institute for Environmental Studies (Mancelona, Michigan) has taken a leading role in environmental studies.

Au Sable began in 1958 as a boys' camp, later became a college biology field-work station and offered environmental education for children, and in 1980 became an environmental institute. Working through the Christian College Coalition, an association of presently eighty-three Christian liberal arts colleges, Au Sable provides college-level courses in environmental studies. It also holds yearly forums and publishes the forum papers, gives retreats and conferences in the area of environmental stewardship for churches, camps, and professional organizations, and provides nature-awareness activities for local students from kindergarten through high school.

Au Sable is a good example of a balanced Christian view that neither abdicates biblical revelation to rewrite the faith, nor glosses over the problem. The 1991 bulletin states the Institute philosophy (in part):

> The basis for the mission of Au Sable Institute is the Bible as the sole authority for faith and practice. The board, faculty, and staff confess that God is exclusive owner of all; that human beings are trustees of that over which they have responsibility. The task and responsibility of human beings is that of stewardship; stewardship is the responsible care and use of the Creation and of its creatures.

Au Sable presents its mission statement as: "The integration of knowledge of the Creation with biblical principles for the purpose of bringing the Christian community and the general public to a better understanding of the Creator and the stewardship of God's creation."

There are bright spots, but as a whole, the Christian church has been slow to respond to ecological issues. The absence of a consistent, thoughtful Christian response has left a vacuum quickly and happily filled by others. Christians must accept some blame, therefore—not for the philosophy behind the exploitation of the earth, but for being silent or waffling when the exploitation has happened.

Christians who get involved in environmental causes will meet passionate, articulate people who hold non-Christian views of nature, humanity, and God. If they're right, why not follow them? If they're wrong, why listen to them? We'll try to answer both those questions next by looking at the logical results of their views.

CHAPTER SIX
DUAL IDOLATRIES

It was on a dreary night of November that
I beheld the accomplishment of my toils.
. . . How can I describe my emotions at
this catastrophe, or how delineate the
wretch whom with such infinite pains and
care I had endeavoured to form?
Mary Shelley, Frankenstein

It is December 3, and already the fourth heavy snowstorm of the season. The third storm was three nights ago. This morning we naturally go to the front door to breathe the clean white air and listen to the snow's silence. Instead we breathe in gasoline fumes and hear roaring motors. The whole neighborhood, the whole *world,* is either manhandling snowblowers or getting their cars unstuck.

We leave town to go skiing in the woods, to glide along on top of the snow and cooperate with nature instead of fighting it. We start out skiing in bright sunshine, only to get caught in another storm. The trail, heavy because it hasn't been groomed since the last storm, fills up and turns even heavier. The temperature is rising and we don't have on "warm" enough wax, so our skis slip back even as we try to slog through the white stuff.

Whether we choose to fight it or cooperate with it, it looks like the snow is going to get us. In the same way, whether we choose to take the technological or the mystical views of nature, both wind up bogging us down in the same condition: we wind up dependent on a *human-centered* solution for a problem of human making.

The Ecological Price Tag

As we saw in Chapter 3, the technological approach to solving environmental problems always balks at the question, "How much is it going to cost?" It is inseparably tied to economics. Barry Commoner, whose career has spanned science and politics, calls such cost-counting a new type of religion.

> In a way, current environmental practice is a return to the medieval approach to disease, when illness—and death itself— was regarded as a debit on life that must be incurred in payment for Original Sin. Now this philosophy has been recast into a more modern form: some level of pollution and some risk to health are the unavoidable price that must be paid for the material benefits of modern technology. (Commoner, *Making Peace with the Planet,* p. 61)

Even as he condemns the ideas of "acceptable levels" of pollution and "risk management" based on weighing environmental damage vs. cost, Commoner winds up favoring a technological approach to "making peace with the planet." And why not? Technology has done wonders for all of us whether we admit it or not. We watch earth-lovers going off to rough it in the woods with their hundred-dollar Primus stoves and three-hundred-dollar backpacks. The white Americans who glibly say Columbus should have stayed home are living deep in comforts inherited directly from Europe.

Hard times ahead?

This year everybody is worried about the economy. Business people across the country are unhappy because they are not making large profits. Working people are unhappy because many of them are *not* working, and those who are working worry about their job security. Consumer debt is at an all-time high, yet economists say unless there's an increase in buying, the country will slip into a deeper recession. They warn us that we need to improve productivity if we are going to stay competitive in the world market.

Locally, a major employer has threatened to leave town, closing the local factory in order to improve its financial status and productivity. A large discount department store recently opened, threatening the security of many smaller local merchants. A friend has taken a job requiring him to be away from home as he travels over five states, only returning home one or two days a week. Others struggle working several part-time jobs trying to make ends meet.

Meanwhile the economy cries out for more and more spending. The ads on TV and in the papers tell us of all the things we "need" and where we can find them. So with credit cards and checkbooks we troop to the malls.

A college senior tells us how expensive it is to go to a private college. He's working two jobs (at minimum wage) and renting a small room off-campus to make ends meet. He wonders how he's going to make it. "And besides," he says almost casually, "I've got a *gigantic* Discover Card bill."

Who's in charge here?

According to Bob Goudzwaard, professor of economics at Free University, Amsterdam, and former Dutch Parliament member, our economic system has turned from good servant to demanding master:

> The production system, initially a willing servant laboring to end our misery, seems to have taken charge. Through its demands for

73

economic growth and rising productivity it tells all of us, whether management or labor, what limits to place on protecting the environment, how many jobs to eliminate, what kind of workers are no longer suitable in the labor system, and what products and necessities must be consumed. And usually we simply listen. (Goudzwaard, *Idols of Our Time,* p. 51)

Like "Audrey II," the plant in *Little Shop of Horrors,* our economy cries "Feed me! Feed me!" and we can only look for an acceptable sacrifice.

Who's the bad guy?

The technical, the scientific, the economic are not villains in themselves. Father John Francis Kavanaugh, Jesuit priest, philosopher, columnist, and film critic, suggests how they become idols:

Many parts of this total [commodity-oriented] world view are not, in themselves, intrinsically damaging to our humanness. The best examples are perhaps scientific and technical intelligence, which, when placed at the service of human dignity, actually exalt and enhance the lives of men and women. It is when the ends-means relationship is inverted, when the scientific model of human knowing becomes imperial or ultimate or when it serves an end other than human dignity, *that the transformation into idolatry takes place.* (Kavanaugh, *Following Christ in a Consumer Society,* p. 43, emphasis added)

There is a "Gross National Byproduct" of lust for economic prosperity. It works like this. We create an idol. We expect it to serve us and do things for us. We wind up serving it, doing whatever it asks, for an idol demands total loyalty and sacrifice.

A Mystical Response

Surely (some say) the answer is to turn from the material to the mystical. If materialistic technology brought about the environmental crisis, mysticism now offers to solve it. But they are both, as we saw in the first chapter, flip sides of the same thing: the lust for power over nature. *Both* are human-centered. Both want to command our full allegiance. Both wind up being idols.

We all remember Mickey Mouse as the "Sorcerer's Apprentice" in *Fantasia*. Mickey tries to ease his water-carrying chore by using unauthorized magic to bring a broom to life. But when he takes a nap, things get out of hand. The broom starts multiplying, Mickey wakes to find an army of brooms flooding everything with water, and he lacks the spell to shut them off.

Science and magic
Familiar as we are with C.S. Lewis as a Christian apologist and novelist, we often overlook that he was by profession a professor of Medieval and Renaissance literature and was well acquainted with the history of those periods. In 1947 he made a fascinating observation on the simultaneous growth of modern science and the magic arts:

> There was very little magic in the Middle Ages: the sixteenth and seventeenth centuries are the high noon of magic. The serious magical endeavour and the serious scientific endeavour are twins: one was sickly and died, the other strong and throve. But they were twins. They were born of the same impulse. . . . For the wise men of old the cardinal problem had been how to conform the soul to reality, and the solution had been knowledge, self-discipline, and virtue. For magic and applied science alike the problem is how to subdue reality to the wishes of men: the solution is a

technique; and both, in the practice of this technique, are ready to do things hitherto regarded as disgusting and impious. . . . [In Francis Bacon's view] The true object is to extend Man's power to the performance of all things possible. He rejects magic because it does not work, but his goal is that of the magician. (Lewis, *The Abolition of Man*, pp. 87-89)

Magic is the attempt to manipulate natural forces to do the magician's bidding. At its root it has the same aim as materialistic technology; the difference is that it taps spirit beings instead of machines to accomplish its goals.

In an interview in the Spiritual Counterfeits Project Journal, James Houston referred to a cult researcher who discovered in his studies that the New Age movement "was not so much a movement of spiritual renewal, as it was a movement based on *bringing the technological model to religious life*" (Houston, "Faith on the Line," *SCP Journal*).

Eugene Peterson observes that going to nature and insisting on getting spiritual experiences from it is only another form of exploiting nature. We visit natural surroundings, and God speaks to us in a way that doesn't usually happen in the church building. So what do we do? We go back again and again, demanding to continue to extract that feeling. "We are not praying but 'using' nature to produce religious feelings."

The practice is common enough to get a fancy name: *homeopathy,* cultivating the feelings/rhythms/actions of divine nature so that divine nature will come under my influence. Nature religion operates on the principle that there is something divine in mountains and rivers, in moon, in sun and stars, in seasons and weather. By "getting into" nature one gets into the divine, participates in the fertility, enlists on the victorious side, experiences immortal ecstasies. There are divine forces in creation that can be offended or appeased. By engaging in the proper rituals and with a little bit of luck, we can manipulate nature for selfish benefit.

This is the origin of the antiprayer called magic. Prayer is *willingness practiced before God;* magic is *willfulness exercised on nature.* (Peterson, *Earth & Altar,* pp. 140-141, emphasis added)

A beautiful, cruel goddess

After his revolutionary *Gaia: A New Look At Life on Earth,* James Lovelock wrote a second book, *The Ages of Gaia,* to try to placate his scientific colleagues that he was not turning from science to mysticism. His final chapter, however, makes it clear that he is calling for a return to the religion of the ancients when earth was worshipped as a goddess.

Unless we rid ourselves of the biblical conception of God and replace it with the fundamentally pagan world view centered on Gaian-Earth worship and goddess spirituality we are surely doomed, says Lovelock. His message is clear; Gaia is our true savior and the God of the Bible is our enemy. (Chevre, "The Gaia Hypothesis: Science, Mythology, and the Desecration of God," *SCP Journal*)

Lovelock's Gaia is hardly depersonalized when he writes that she is

stern and tough, always keeping the world warm for those who obey the rules, but ruthless in her destruction of those who transgress. . . . If humans stand in the way of this, we shall be eliminated with as little pity as would be shown by the microbrain of an intercontinental ballistic nuclear missile in full flight to its target. (Lovelock, *The Ages of Gaia: A Biography of Our Living Earth,* p. 212)

Recently we were drawn to an attractive book called *To Care for the Earth.* The author, Sean McDonagh, is the Irish Catholic missionary we mentioned earlier who worked in the Philippines for many years. We lived in a Catholic town in Northern Ireland and were interested in his perspective. Much of his book is compassionate and creative. It is also absolutist in its vision for what must be:

> This vision of an evolving Earth must today become *the norm of what is real and worth striving for* within every institution on the planet. Human beings must enter as creatively as possible into the processes of the planet *in order to discern the true role of the human* within the Earth's story. The emergent story will give the human community *basic norms* to guide the human-Earth relationship in a way that will be mutually enriching and enhancing. These norms *must be enshrined in our political, economic, social, commercial and religious institutions* so that these enhance the Earth community and do not impoverish it. (McDonagh, *To Care for the Earth,* p. 81, emphasis added)

It is frightening to imagine the despotism visited on society if people who believe these things are in power. They will even define for us what it means to be human. Living in fear of elimination by the goddess, they will do anything to enforce humanity's worldwide cooperation with her. Those who do not bow to her are obviously endangering all of humankind by courting her wrath. The parallel to paganism is obvious.

The earth-centered ecological view talks much of cultural pluralism and tolerance. But behind it is an absolutism that when enforced will naturally lead to totalitarianism.

Who will do the enforcing? People who think "right." Even deep ecology winds up being human-centered because there is no one else to enforce the democracy of the biosphere. The necessary reduction of human population (which Arne Naess and George Sessions say the flourishing of nonhuman life "requires") can only be achieved by technology. Unless, of course, they are willing to reduce the population by nature's way, which is starvation.

Deep Questions Remain

Arne Naess, who originated the term "deep ecology," answered the objection that things must kill each other to live by saying that all living things have the *right* to live, but that at times there are *competing* rights to live, and then choices must be made.

As criteria in the case of competing claims between, for instance, poisonous snakes and small children in a playground, Naess suggests *vitalness* and *nearness:* the more vital interest has priority over the less vital, and the nearer has priority over the more remote—"in space, time, culture, or species" (Richards, "The Nature-Culture Dilemma," *Breakthrough*).

The human children, then, have a more "vital" right to live than the snakes do. But certainly not from the snakes' point of view. They would regard all those trampling human feet as a legitimate threat to their environment, not to mention their heads. If we are going to vote for the children over the snakes—if we are even going to assume that we have the right to vote—then we are inescapably anthropocentric.

Somebody must decide. And ultimately even the deep ecologist says *humanity* must decide. It is, after all, human beings who write the deep ecology books and state what is right and wrong. To whom do they write the books? Other humans.

Humanity's place of dominion seems written into the way things are. Even the Gaia hypothesis elevates humanity as the consciousness of Gaia. She had not even gotten a good look at herself until human-made spacecraft let us back away far enough.

The snakes on the playground raise the very important issue of *who decided* deep ecology's "two ultimate norms" (self-realization and biocentric equality) in the first place. You'll recall that Bill Devall and George Sessions explain they are "arrived at by the deep questioning process and reveal the importance of moving to the philosophical and religious level of wisdom. They cannot be validated, of course, by the methodology of modern science based on its usual mechanistic assumptions and its very narrow definition of data" (Devall and Sessions, *Deep Ecology,* p. 66).

If the norms of self-realization and biocentric equality are arrived at by deep questioning, of whom are the questions asked? Who provides the answers? Not the scientists in the lab; they are specifically locked out. Then what is the source of the "wisdom" reached at the "philosophical and religious" level? If the norms cannot be validated by science, is there any standard by which they can be validated? They are simply stated as norms by which all other ideas are validated or not.

Apparently it is the Self who answers these "deep questionings" and it is the Self, the All, which is the source of the knowledge. But the All includes many things not acceptable to the deep ecologist. If there are no boundaries, who can say that pure air is right and pollution is wrong? What's the difference between a beaver dam and Hoover dam?

Where are the answers?

We instinctively shrink from the person who announces, "God told me." For some time American society has relegated that phrase to nut cases. Christian politicians such as Pat Robertson and Jimmy Carter carefully avoided saying, "God told me to run for President" (even though we hope as committed Christians they would not run *unless* they were led by God to do it). It is just about impossible to talk to someone who announces, "God told me." There is no discussion. The person *knows*.

As Christians we sometimes have that experience, when God tells us to do something, when we *know*. We can't explain it; we just know. No one understands, or perhaps only a few understand, but we have to obey even if it makes no sense to anyone else.

So we find no fault with intuitive knowledge in and of itself. It has been the voice of prophecy and creativity and inspiration throughout God's dealings with people.

Deep ecology, with its purely intuitive "norms"—untestable, inarguable—lifts itself in such a prophetic position. It announces, "God told me"—"God" being not a Person but the incontrovertible voice of Self, which is also the great All.

The difference is that deep ecology operates within a *closed system* just as materialistic technology does. All there is, is the "All" of Earth (or the Universe, but their concern is really for Earth's ecology). There is no personal God who can reveal or intervene or speak or save; there is only the living organism of the planet. If that is true, our resources are "limited" in ways the ecologists never dreamed of. The Earth is its own God and it is She who gives the orders.

> But has anything of substance changed if an ethics of progress has merely been transformed into an ethics of survival? This question is decisive because in both types of ethics it is a system—either of progress or of survival—that provides the norms for good or evil. (Goudzwaard, *Capitalism & Progress*, p. 128)

So earth's ecology needs a systemic solution; it must be treated as a whole system. But who does the treating?

Sailing with Captain Nemo

One Thanksgiving about ten years ago we watched a made-for-TV movie called (if memory is right) "Goliath Awaits." Divers discover a luxury ocean liner that went down in World War II—and it's still full of live people! They're living it up down there in apparent bliss, eating aquaculture-grown food, breathing oxygen from hanging gardens, and dancing to '40s tunes like "Somewhere Over the Rainbow" (apparently no composers went down with the ship). It's a totally self-sustaining, self-contained system run by the brilliant, dictatorial captain.

The catch is, the system cannot tolerate unproductive people. If anyone is sick or injured and can't work, the person is injected with a quick-acting fatal disease.

On the *Nautilus,* Captain Nemo was master of his own undersea kingdom. "Ah, sir," he said to Monsieur Aronnax, "live—live in the bosom of the waters! There only is independence! There I recognise no masters! There I am free!" But there no one else was free; all were prisoners doomed never to leave the *Nautilus*. Nemo was sole lord of his self-contained domain:

> I am not what you call a civilised man! I have done with society entirely. . . . I do not therefore obey its laws, and I desire you never to allude to them before me again! (Verne, *Twenty Thousand Leagues Under the Sea,* pp. 66, 72)

If the earth is a closed system that needs a systemic treatment, who will decide on the treatment? Who will administer it? If the whole earth is to be treated with one medicine, what happens to dissenters who don't want to take the medicine? Like *Goliath* and the *Nautilus*—and like the old Moody Science Film "City of the Bees"—there is no mercy for the one who will not cooperate. That one is disposed of. In a closed, finite system run by a dictator, there can be no mercy. Who dares argue with the Earth Goddess who will shed us all like fleas if we displease her?

Lost: The Christian base

Francis Schaeffer maintained that we enjoy certain freedoms that came out of our society's previous "Christian consensus"; that is, though not everyone in the United States was a committed Christian, we had commonly held ideas of human dignity and responsibility that made our civil freedoms possible.

> When these freedoms are separated from the Christian base, however, they become a force of destruction leading to chaos. When this happens, as it has today, then, to quote Eric Hoffer . . . "When freedom destroys order, the yearning for order will destroy freedom."
> *At that point the words left or right will make no difference.*

They are only two roads to the same end. There is no difference between an authoritarian government from the right or the left: the results are the same. An elite, an authoritarianism as such, will gradually force form on society so that it will not go on to chaos. And most people will accept it—from the desire for personal peace and affluence, from apathy, and from the yearning for order to assure the functioning of some political system, business, and the affairs of daily life. That is just what Rome did with Caesar Augustus. (Schaeffer, *How Should We Then Live?* p. 245, emphasis added)

C.S. Lewis had sounded the same warning nearly thirty years earlier:

What we call Man's power over Nature turns out to be a power exercised by some men over other men with Nature as its instrument. . . . Each new power won *by* man is a power *over* man as well. Each advance leaves him weaker as well as stronger. In every victory, besides being the general who triumphs, he is also the prisoner who follows the triumphal car. . . .

The final stage is come when Man by eugenics, by prenatal conditioning, and by an education and propaganda based on a perfect applied psychology, has obtained full control over himself. *Human* nature will be the last part of Nature to surrender to Man. The battle will then be won. . . . But who, precisely, will have won it? (Lewis, *The Abolition of Man,* pp. 69, 71-72)

If this chapter sounds pessimistic, that's only because the technological and the mystical views of ecology rest on a shaky base—sinful human beings. If there is going to be hope for the earth (and for us) there must be another base for ecology. There must be something eternal and dependable on which to build our philosophy of nature.

That is what we will attempt to build in the second half of this book.

PART TWO
RESTORING THE VISION

CHAPTER SEVEN
GOD AND CREATION

And God stepped out on space,
And He looked around and said,
"I'm lonely.
I'll make me a world."
James Weldon Johnson, "The Creation"

Wake-up was at 4 A.M. on the archaeological dig at Tell Gezer, Israel. After graham crackers with peanut butter and jelly, the crew would head east from camp to the dig site a short distance away. Every morning we walked toward a flaming sunrise, each unique in its own different brilliance.

Once a dig member stopped a moment to stare. His mind went back to the biblical people whose city we were violating with our pickaxes every day.

"Maybe there was a God—back then," he murmured. Then he added, "And even if there wasn't, I see why people who lived here thought there was."

Evidence for the Unseen

Not only in Palestine has the natural world pointed to a Person behind it all. In cultures all over the world, people have considered nature and asked, "Where did it come from?"

In hospital recovering from war wounds and sickness, the young atheist C.S. Lewis had the luxury of time to read and think about evidences for God. His friend Arthur Greeves suggested to him that some evidence for the existence of God could be found in the beauty of the natural world.

Lewis became curious about precisely *where* the "beauty" of a tree resides. In purely physical terms, when you look at a tree, light waves bouncing off it produce reactions in the nerves of your eye, carrying sensations of color and shape to your brain. He asked:

How then does the beauty of the tree arise? Shape, size, color, touch, and the like are simply the names we call our sensations, and no amount of study of them can ever bring us to the notion of beauty in the tree. Beauty must therefore arise from some non-material relation between the tree and myself.

Though Lewis was not yet ready to attribute such a "nonmaterial relation" to a personal God, he had taken "a long step upward for the atheist" (Gilbert and Kilby, *C.S. Lewis: Images of His World,* pp. 17-18).

Lewis's writings after he became a Christian, particularly *The Abolition of Man,* show he came to believe there *is* something intrinsically good and beautiful in the objective world external to our feelings. What's interesting in his hospital-bound thoughts is that beauty *in* nature led him logically to the possibility of reality *beyond* nature.

The One behind it all
Some of us have been fortunate enough to sing Haydn's oratorio "Creation," and we have all heard its text from Psalm 19: "The

heavens are telling the glory of God/the wonder of his love displays the firmament!"

If creation does not speak in human language, how does it "tell" the glory of God? You've probably sung Joseph Addison's paraphrase of Psalm 19 (which is also set to Haydn's music):

What though no real voice nor sound
Amid the radiant orbs be found?
In reason's ear they all rejoice,
And utter forth a glorious voice;
Forever singing as they shine,
"The hand that made us is divine."

Reason tells us that the natural world we observe is not an accident but is made by Someone. The psalmist who marveled at creation's "voice" was also familiar with God's written Law. For those without the Scriptures, nature and conscience are the primary revealers of God. "For since the creation of the world God's invisible qualities—his eternal power and divine nature—have been clearly seen, being understood *from what has been made,* so that men are without excuse" (Rom. 1:20, emphasis added).

Starting with Creation

Nature proclaims to Jew and Gentile that God made it. Therefore all Christians concerned for ecology must be creationists. By "creationists" we don't refer to any theory of specifically *when* or *how* God created. We mean that, first of all, we must acknowledge that God *did* create everything, and we will never relate to creation as we should if we ignore the fact of his creation.

We can enumerate endangered species and analyze oil spills, protest nuclear waste dumps and protect wilderness areas, but if we see this earth *only* as a conglomeration of such things, we misunderstand its essence. If we want to construct a genuinely Christian ecology, we must begin by looking at the earth—and indeed the universe—*as something that is really here made by a Person who is really here*. Without that Person, none of it would exist. Without that Person, none of it has meaning.

Our Scriptures begin, "In the beginning God created the heavens and the earth" (Gen. 1:1). There is not a tremor of an apology for such an authoritative statement, and no proof; it is simply stated as fact. It does not say when, why, or how. But it says *who*.

The ancient Hebrews chanted it together:

O give thanks to the Lord of lords:
> for his mercy endureth for ever.
To him who alone doeth great wonders:
> for his mercy endureth for ever.
To him that by wisdom made the heavens:
> for his mercy endureth for ever.
To him that stretched out the earth above the waters:
> for his mercy endureth for ever.
To him that made great lights:
> for his mercy endureth for ever.
The sun to rule by day:
> for his mercy endureth for ever.
The moon and stars to rule by night:
> for his mercy endureth for ever. (Ps. 136:3-9, KJV)

Wisdom, the power before the ages

The Lord "by wisdom" made the heavens, the psalm says. In Proverbs 8, Wisdom is personified as One who existed from the beginning, active in creation:

The Lord brought me forth as the first of his works,
> before his deeds of old;
I was appointed from eternity,

from the beginning, before the world began.
When there were no oceans, I was given birth,
    when there were no springs abounding with water;
before the mountains were settled in place,
    before the hills, I was given birth,
before he made the earth or its fields
    or any of the dust of the world.
I was there when he set the heavens in place,
    when he marked out the horizon on the face of the deep,
when he established the clouds above
    and fixed securely the foundations of the deep,
when he gave the sea its boundary
    so the waters would not overstep his command,
and when he marked out the foundations of the earth.
    Then I was the craftsman at his side.
I was filled with delight day after day,
    rejoicing always in his presence,
rejoicing in his whole world
    and delighting in mankind. (Prov. 8:22-31)

Who is this "Wisdom" who claims to be much more than an abstract concept, who claims to have been involved in creation?

In the New Testament, the writer of the book of Hebrews begins his long, circular argument for Christ's supremacy over all other priests and sacrifices by saying: "In many and various ways God spoke of old to our fathers by the prophets; but in these last days he has spoken to us by a Son, whom he appointed the heir of all things, through whom also he created the world" (Heb. 1:1-2, RSV, emphasis added). It sounds almost tagged on, a throw-away line: oh, and by the way, through him God made the world.

Christ is the Word, the *Logos,* through whom God made everything. We know that he is intimately involved in this physical world because he "became flesh and made his dwelling among us" (John 1:14). But long before he became a man to suffer here, he was involved with joy in making this world.

> The figure of "the master workman," rejoicing, even *playing* in the bringing-forth of the diverse creation, equal and sharing equally in that work of creation, is, from the Christian perspective, a clear anticipation of Christ the Word without whom nothing was made. (Wilkinson, "Cosmic Christology and the Christian's Role in Creation," *Christian Scholar's Review*)

The Christians at Colossae were threatened by the gnostic idea that a holy God could not possibly have created the evil material world. Paul countered that idea when he wrote to them that Christ is "the image of the invisible God, the firstborn over all creation. For by him all things were created: things in heaven and on earth, visible and invisible, whether thrones or powers or rulers or authorities; all things were created by him and for him" (Col. 1:15-16). John, who had seen and touched the human person Jesus, acknowledged that this One who had walked the earth was actually Creator. "Through him all things were made; without him nothing was made that has been made" (John 1:3).

Those are tremendous claims to be made of Jesus, the same Jesus who "humbled himself and became obedient to death" (Phil. 2:8). It's vital to see that this claim of Creatorship *is* made of the historical Jesus, for the New Testament writers (unlike many modern environmentalists) know nothing of any "Christ" outside of the person who was incarnate as Jesus of Nazareth, who was born in a city we can identify today and was crucified and rose in a city we can identify today, during the political reign of certain persons we know by name.

Christ the Wisdom of God has set the example of intimate, sacrificial involvement with earth. He is God incarnate, taking on the flesh of a human creature, identifying himself with us and creation and in this way declaring over again (as in Genesis) that "it is good."

Whereas a one-sided view of either God's transcendence or immanence compounds our problems, a biblical combination of both points the way through our dilemmas. If we stress only God's immanence (God's presence in the world), we land in pantheism where everything is divine and good as it is. If we talk only about God's transcendence (God's radical distinctiveness from creation), we may end up seeing nature as a mere tool to be used at human whim. The biblical God is both immanent and transcendent. (Ronald J. Sider, "Green Theology," *ESA Advocate,* p. 1)

Our Foundation: Love for God

Any ecology that attempts to be Christian must start with our relationship to a personal God who is Creator. Our unique beginning point distinguishes our ecology from others, which start with the need to save the earth and construct or adapt a religion to fit that need.

If we start with saving the earth and try either to reason out or to feel out a God who can do it for us, we wind up remaking God either in *our* image or in the *earth's* image. Instead, we must first love and honor God the Creator in order to respect his world rightly.

Right away objections can be raised. What about the "dig" volunteer watching the sun rise over Tell Gezer, and the young Lewis in the hospital? What about the many people who first appreciate nature and through it are led to believe in God? Don't they love nature *first,* then through nature come to love God?

That's true, but the process can't *end* there.

We may come to believe in God through loving nature. But once we begin to know God, we must turn around and reevaluate how we treat everything else (the natural world, other people) in the light of who God is. God the Creator, not nature, becomes our ultimate reference point.

If nature rather than God is our reference point, our way of looking at the world (including our ecology) will be perverted. It may take the form of a greedy love of earth's treasures. Or it may be an ascetic scorning of the good earth. Or it may be a pantheistic worship of nature for nature's sake. Whatever it is, it will not be a genuinely Christian ecology.

Our role in the cosmos

After we have concluded that God made everything, including ourselves, we humans can't leave it at that. Something in our minds and hearts wants to ask a more personal question: What are *we* doing here? Are we brainy apes who will someday be superseded by brainier apes—or dolphins? Are we (as some say) a blight on it all, best gotten rid of? Or do we have a special place here and a special job to do?

Of the entire body of literature that Christians call the Bible, nothing is more troubling to secular ecologists (even some Christian ecologists) than God's command in Genesis 1:28:

> Be fruitful and increase in number; fill the earth and subdue it. Rule over the fish of the sea and the birds of the air and over every living creature that moves on the ground.

The command is more popularly known in the KJV: "Be fruitful, and multiply, and replenish the earth, and subdue it: and have dominion over the fish of the sea, and over the fowl of the air, and over every living thing that moveth upon the earth."

It's that phrase "have dominion" that puts people off. In any environmental discussion there's no quicker way to raise the tension level in the room than to refer to that verse. Lots of people who know little else about the Bible (and you start meeting them as soon as you start discussing ecology with the world at large) know *that* verse and blame earth's problems directly on it.

Put the kabash on it? The first humans were told to do five things: Be fruitful, multiply, fill the earth, subdue it, and rule over living creatures.

The first three commands are not disputed much, as commands logically given to early humanity (though there is plenty of modern argument about whether it's time for humanity to cut back on "being fruitful, multiplying, and filling the earth"). The tension-causer, the *offense* to so many environmentalists, is in the last two commands: subdue the earth and rule over other life. They are the ammunition in the argument that Christianity has nothing good to say about ecology and in fact is largely to blame for the problem.

> Dominion has come to represent everything those seeking to be responsible "stewards" object to: hierarchical power relations; a humanocentrism that allows nature no independent integrity; ownership of and property rights over natural resources; and divine authorization for exploitative use of the earth and its limited resources. (Steffen, "In Defense of Dominion")

The Hebrew words of Genesis 1:28 are muscular words. "Subdue" is in Hebrew *kabash,* as in "he really put the kabash on my idea." To "rule" (KJV "have dominion") is *radah,* to "tread down" or "trample," also to "govern, rule." Nothing wishy-washy about these commands of God to the first humans.

How should Christians deal with Genesis 1:28? It is there; we cannot excise it from the Bible. We cannot write it off as "Old Testament law" because it is so obviously a basic mandate given to all humanity. We have no right to reinterpret it casually to fit popular preferences. And we dare not ignore it, because it reports the very words of God.

Therefore—if we are going to be honest—we have no choice but to look closely at this passage and dig into what it means, whether or not we like what is there.

Barefoot in the grass. After years of having his feet "shod from dawn to dark, rubber boots for the barn and leather ones for the field," Mike Brost quit dairy farming and began going barefoot. Life is very different for Mike and his feet now:

A hike in the woods becomes the careful placement of one foot in front of the other. This brings out the small details in the path. *The little things the shod foot tramples, the bare foot caresses lightly.* . . . The outdoors are not meant to be left to an elite group with high-priced footwear. Primitive people have walked the earth since the beginning with only the soles of their feet between them and terra firma. (Brost, in *Northern View*, emphasis added)

Perhaps Brost's insight tempers a little the command to Adam and Eve to "trample" the earth. Shoeless, the earliest humans could not have "trampled" very hard on anything.

But of course the command to trample was given with full knowledge that humanity would put on shoes soon enough. There is no indication that the command to subdue the earth was rescinded when humanity started wearing sandals, moccasins, boots, Florsheims, and Reeboks. The command was apparently meant for humankind in general, forever. It was an inescapable condition of being human. (Some maintain that the command to have dominion *was* rescinded after the flood. In Genesis 9:1 God repeats to Noah and his sons the commands to "be fruitful and increase in number and fill the earth"; nothing is said about the other two commands, to subdue and rule. However, God also says [9:2] that living creatures will fear mankind and that "they are given into your hands." It certainly sounds like a continuation of rule and dominion.)

In the image of God. What's often missed in the discussion of dominion is that Genesis 1:28 is not the *beginning* of what God had to say about the matter. We cannot comprehend God's purposes, but the revelation of Scripture does give us some finite glimpses into the infinite mind of God. Genesis 1:26 lets us in on what God considered *before* he made humanity and gave them the command to have dominion. After the rest of creation was finished, God said:

Let us make man in our image, in our likeness, and let them rule over the fish of the sea and the birds of the air, over the livestock, over all the earth, and over all the creatures that move along the ground. (Gen. 1:26)

Then "God created man in his own image, in the image of God he created him; male and female he created them" (Gen. 1:27).

Our *function,* to rule and have dominion over the earth, grows directly out of our *position,* which is that we are made "in the image of God." Our call to *act* here on earth (by exercising dominion) comes out of *who* we are, beings created in the "image of God."

Paul picked up the same theme in the New Testament when he wrote, "We are therefore Christ's ambassadors" (2 Cor. 5:20). As ambassadors we are never authorized to act independently of God's will; as his representatives we are authorized to act only in obedience to him.

The *Interpreter's Dictionary of the Bible* tells us that in the use of the word "image"

the intention is not to define man's essence or God's nature, but rather to indicate *man's task and his relationship to God.* As *God's living image on earth,* man is to act as his representative. He is the administrator of God's works. Hence the thought quickly moves from the "image" to the announcement that God has given man a special blessing and has commanded him to exercise dominion over the earth. (Anderson, "Creation," *The Interpreter's Dictionary of the Bible,* emphasis added)

Tending the garden. Dominion is neither the *first* word nor the *last* word in the creation story on humanity's relationship to the earth. "The LORD God took the man and put him in the Garden of Eden to work it and take care of it" (Gen. 2:15). Here is a fuller picture of *how* humanity is to exercise dominion over the earth.

Adam was told to *work* or till the garden. The Hebrew word is *abad,* "to till," or "to serve."

If we are to "serve" the earth, does that mean creation is our master? E. Calvin Beisner was alarmed by such an idea and wrote

97

that "to make man subservient to the earth is to turn the purpose of God in creation on its head" (Beisner, *Prospects for Growth,* p. 163). Certainly earth is not to be "served" as an idol. But perhaps Beisner misses the point of Adam's "service."

Scripture provides the perfect example of the kind of "service" Adam was meant to do. It is given by the life of Jesus.

When the disciples were arguing about who was the greatest, Jesus said to them, "The kings of the Gentiles lord it over them; and those who exercise authority over them call themselves Benefactors. But you are not to be like that. Instead, the greatest among you should be like the youngest, and the one who rules like the one who serves." And he added pointedly, "I am among you as one who serves" (Luke 22:25-27).

We are to have dominion over the earth, but it is a dominion turned *upside down* from the view of the world. Jesus' own life is our example of how we are to carry out our role of dominion, "For even the Son of Man did not come to be served, but to serve" (Mark 10:45).

Stewards of the Earth

In Genesis 2:15 Adam was also told to "take care of" the earth. Here the word *shamar* is used, "to guard or be vigilant for the sake of another."

"Stewardship," which we often relate only to pledging to the church budget once a year, really means "the care of things not our own." Right from the beginning, the care of the earth was the most basic example of stewardship. We are to be stewards of the earth, taking good care of it for the sake of its real owner.

Jesus told several parables about stewardship. In most of them, a master goes away and leaves certain things in the care of servants who act either wisely or unwisely. Then the master returns. "Who then is the faithful and wise servant," he asks, "whom the master has put in charge of the servants in his household to give them their food at the proper time? It will be good for that servant whose master finds him doing so when he returns" (Matt. 24:45-46). The wise servant recognizes that the household is not his and that his job is to take good care of it until the master returns.

In *abad* we are responsible to the earth itself to be its servant. In *shamar* we are responsible to the true owner of the earth, to God himself. There is no question which responsibility is the ultimate one, for God the Creator is greater than the earth he created.

Part of nature
We relate to the natural world as God's special representatives, created in God's image. At the same time we cannot look at ourselves as *totally* different from the rest of creation. Such separation tempts us to treat nature like a mere machine or even worse. We respect a good machine or tool that does its job well, but our response to it is primarily utilitarian. We have no qualms about discarding it once it fails to function properly or we find a better one.

> The Hebrew Scriptures of Judaism have no word for "the environment." Neither do they have a word for "nature" or "the Creation." They do not provide for an objective environment set apart from human beings. This recognizes that we too are creatures and thus are *part,* and not *apart.* Thus, modern Jewish and Christian religions inherit the concept that everything comprises an orderly and harmonious whole—a whole that in later Jewish tradition and in the Christian scriptures is designated as "the Creation." (De-Witt, "The Religious Foundations of Ecology," *The Mother Earth Handbook*)

In many of the Psalms we are called to worship God *right along with* the rest of creation. In Psalm 148, kings, princes, young people, old people, all are called to praise God along with the sun and moon, the wild animals, the mountains and clouds and lightning. In Psalm 104 we join the rest of creation waiting on the Lord to provide for us:

"He makes grass to grow for the cattle, and plants for man to cultivate—bringing forth food from the earth: wine that gladdens the heart of man, oil to make his face shine, and bread that sustains his heart" (Ps. 104:14-15).

Our dominion *over* nature does not cancel out our being *part* of nature. We share in its "creatureness" and its dependence on God; we raise our voices with it in praise to our Creator. We are made of its very dust. "The LORD God formed the man from the dust of the ground and breathed into his nostrils the breath of life, and the man became a *living being*" (Gen. 2:7, emphasis added). That is the same word, *nefesh*, used in Genesis 1:20, 24, and 28 to describe other living creatures.

How easy it is to go along barely noticing the creation—or to notice it for its own beauty, snapping pictures of the scenery, but never thinking of God who made it. If we are part of the creation, we raise our hearts and voices with it and allow it to lead us into experiences of worship.

That may be difficult on the hiking trail when our mouths are full of mosquitoes or in the park when the picnic basket is full of ants. But if we let it happen, we will be led naturally into times of worship when we realize our creaturehood, when we know we do not deserve the good world God is showing us. Maybe being bested by insignificant ants and mosquitoes shows us our human limitations—and after all, the bugs have to make a living, too.

Not only part of nature

It's important to see ourselves as part of nature. It is equally important that we see ourselves as not *only* another species of *nefesh*. According to Genesis 1:28, we are more than that; we are also *over* the rest of creation. We cannot lower ourselves to be on equal footing with the rabbits or the elephants or the ferns or the birches. To do so would be to diminish our humanity.

There is no such thing as "biocentric equality" or biological democracy, and it is not arrogance (or "speciesism") for Christians to say so. To recognize our uniqueness is to agree with God's revelation of our nature and purpose. True arrogance is to ignore God's revelation and reinterpret humanity as something God never intended us to be.

It is actually self-defeating for environmentalists to claim that we humans are only another species. To say that we are just another "Occupant" of a niche in the natural world actually cuts the heart out of environmental responsibility. The reason? If we are only "part of nature," then we cannot be faulted for any of our actions, no matter how much they damage other parts of nature.

After all, we do not fault a wolf for killing a rabbit, or a rabbit for destroying plant roots as it digs its burrow. The beaver who builds a dam does not consider the fate of the loon whose nest, precisely at the water's edge, will be destroyed if the water rises. Nor does it consider the fate of the waterlogged trees, except its favorite, the aspen, on which it depends for food and shelter. All those creatures act according to their nature. So do we inventive humans when our minds teem with new ideas and we create new ways of extracting and using the resources of the earth.

By singling out human beings for condemnation, environmentalists confess along with Christians that something *different,* something *higher,* should be expected of us. The rabbit and the beaver and the wolf can be excused for what they destroy, but we ought to know better.

Nature's Inherent Value

Our dominion is no excuse for considering ourselves little gods. Even if there were no human beings, God's creation has its own value totally apart from humanity. Five different times Genesis declares, "And God saw that it was good," before humanity is even mentioned. God stopped Job's complaints not by answering his questions but by pointing out the wonders of the natural world he had made when Job wasn't even around (Job 38–41). "The morning stars sang together and all the angels shouted for joy" when God laid the cornerstone of the earth's foundation (Job 38:7).

If there should be any question about creation having value apart from humanity, Paul puts it straight. Of Jesus Christ he writes, "For by him all things were created: things in heaven and on earth, visible and invisible, whether thrones or powers or rulers or authorities; all things were created by him and for him" (Col. 1:15). There can be no doubt, "all things" are created not for us but for the Lord. Yet we have our place here.

Camped on the floor of a remote canyon, on a tiny island where a creek divided, sleeping on hard ground under cold stars, Paul Gruchow saw himself diminished before the universe, felt "the great, unaccountable luck of being alive at that moment in that place, I who had so little claim on the universe." But exactly where did that exalted feeling come from?

> It was, I recognized, a gift of the great civilization I had left behind that I felt this joy. It was the gift of contrast, of comparison, the gift of an abundance sufficient to allow me to indulge in the possibility of beauty where there was no commercial utility. When the earth was still largely a wilderness and the rare thing was a place tamed and made safe for human habitation, there was no beauty or joy of this kind in wildness. When every day was still a struggle for survival, there was no leisure for getting away from it all. (Gruchow, *The Necessity of Empty Places*, p. 92)

The very fact of human civilization gives us appreciation for the wildness of the places civilization has not reached. Both have their place. God "fashioned and made the earth, he founded it; he did not create it to be empty, but formed it to be inhabited" (Isa. 45:18). We who live here have a special place and a special responsibility.

And nothing should be more obvious than that something has gone wrong somewhere.

CHAPTER EIGHT
FALLEN AND REDEEMED

That something is everywhere
and always amiss is part of
the very stuff of creation.
Annie Dillard, **Pilgrim at Tinker Creek**

A cormorant stands on an offshore rock, holding its wings out wide. The bird looks like it's about to take off, but it keeps standing there with wings spread to the afternoon sun.

You've heard the expression "like water off a duck's back"? You'll never hear "like water off a cormorant's back." Cormorants' feathers lack the oil that makes ducks float. The dark fish-eating birds can swim submerged with only their heads and long necks sticking out of the water, snakelike. But they'll sink if they don't come out now and then to dry their waterlogged feathers.

It is a bright, warm day. For a while we watch the sunning bird through binoculars. Over the roar of motorboats and the splashes and yells of children swimming, an insidious *chop-chop-chop* sound gradually fills the air. It's the Coast Guard helicopter that recently passed offshore; it has come back. It sweeps low over the water, flies away up the lakeshore, comes back again. They are searching for somebody.

Not everyone who goes into the cold waters of Lake Superior comes out to dry his feathers. The news comes later: a man went fishing alone, and next morning his boat washed up on shore empty. His body was not found for a week.

Read the Fine Print

The lake that provides fish for the sunning cormorant took a human life. Does it make any difference to the lake? Does it care?

A coupon for a "green" all-purpose cleaner (literally and figuratively) assures us it's "non-toxic, biodegradable, non-abrasive, environmentally safe." This is a cleaner you can use in harmony with the natural world.

But don't miss the ominous note in the fine print. When you purchase this cleaner, the maker will donate a percentage of the price to the American Red Cross Disaster Relief Fund. Use this product and you'll help the victims of earthquakes, hurricanes, floods, and tornadoes.

We long to be partners with the natural world. We ease ourselves up to it, admire it, treat it with respect, even revere it. And all the time it can turn around and wipe us out without a twinge of conscience.

You've heard about "the wreck of the *Edmund Fitzgerald*" in a November gale, but every year we've lived here, summer or winter, someone has died in the bay. In summer they go fishing or swimming and don't come back. In winter they snowmobile across the ice and break through.

The lake is impartial, indifferent, and unforgiving. So is all of nature, beneath its seductive beauty. We can learn to cooperate with it, and we can coerce it to some degree, but we can never gain its favoritism. A hurricane doesn't stop to ask us whether we're exploiters or environmentalists.

Wastefulness, death

"The universal chomp," Annie Dillard calls it in *Pilgrim at Tinker Creek*—the wastefulness and rampant death in the world. Some animals eat their own young; some eat their parents or their mates. Among the lower animals, billions of eggs are laid and lost. "If an aphid lays a million eggs," she says, "several might survive. Now, my right hand, in all its human cunning, could not make one aphid in a thousand years. But these aphid eggs—which run less than a dime a dozen, which run absolutely free—can make aphids as effortlessly as the sea makes waves. Wonderful things, wasted. It's a wretched system."

When we think about it, we are appalled; yet plainly it's the way things are. Dillard concludes that there are two possibilities: This is a cruel and terrible world, in which case we are right to be shocked by its cruelty; or this is a beautiful and perfect world, in which case *we* are warped to think that *it* is warped. "Either this world, my mother, is a monster, or I myself am a freak" (Dillard, *Pilgrim at Tinker Creek,* pp. 159-181).

We live our lives in such ambivalence toward nature that when it turns a domesticated face to us, we're surprised and unnerved.

Waiting for a handout

We drove into Sibley Provincial Park, the "Sleeping Giant" peninsula that wraps around the harbor of Thunder Bay, Ontario. At what looked like a trailhead we got out of the car to read a small-print sign. A minute later, when we turned back, a fox was waiting for us by the car.

He sat with his tail curled around him, a polite guest waiting for the soup course. When shooed away he went a few steps and sat down again, patient. He was that accustomed to humans in the park feeding him. His fur looked terrible; we wondered what junk food he'd been living on all summer.

Further into the park, deer wandered onto the road and watched our car with that same expectant "food" look. When the car didn't stop, they turned and moved down the road ahead of it like a flock of leggy brown sheep.

Later, on a more remote trail, the animals seemed to be keeping their normal distance—till a ruffed grouse hen came wandering up the path toward us, picking at the heads of weeds.

You need to know that ruffed grouse are shy birds. They normally spot you before you spot them and startle you by taking off with a thunder of wings. And here came this grouse hen clucking along directly toward us, eating her seeds. She paused, looked at us with mild curiosity, then resumed clucking and picking almost up to our feet before casually turning off into the weeds.

A break in the chain

Such nonchalant meetings with wild creatures are not only unnerving, they're a little disappointing. The stealth and surprise, the *fun,* goes out of spotting a wild animal when it walks right up to you. It's like those bears at Yellowstone that used to swarm all over people's cars. There's something *unnatural* about getting so close to wild animals so easily. Every child raised near the woods knows that if a wild animal approaches you like a pet, tame and friendly, it's dangerous; there's something wrong with it.

Even at Sleeping Giant, the wild animals are not displaying true friendship to humans. They're like the chipmunk that begs at your campsite or the gulls that assault your picnic table, or those Yellowstone bears. The animals have trained us dumb humans to be their food source. In the *real* world there is an unbridgeable gulf between us and wild animals.

Haven't you felt it? You watch squirrels and birds and rabbits hopping around your yard peacefully coexisting with each other. But try to approach them—you, a fellow creature—and they flee.

What's going on? If we are "part of" nature, then why does nature not regard us as part of itself? Why does it shun us, or flee from us, or injure us even when we mean it no harm?

Out of Balance?

The split between humanity and the rest of nature started with the first humans' first exploitation of the natural world.

In the garden, Adam and Eve enjoyed freedoms and pleasures and meaningful work in the perfect environment where they had been placed by God. They were given only one restriction: to refrain from eating the fruit of the tree of the knowledge of good and evil.

But it was not enough for Adam and Eve to enjoy looking at the tree while they left it to grow in peace in God's garden. "The lust of the flesh, and the lust of the eyes, and the pride of life" got hold of them (1 John 2:16, KJV). They craved the tree for what it could *do* for them.

The first seed of temptation was planted when the serpent asked, "Did God really say, 'You must not eat from any tree in the garden?'" (Gen. 3:1). The serpent was wise enough to know that a direct attack on God would meet with resistance. A well-placed question (that exaggerated God's restrictions) could plant a seed of doubt, and with proper nurture it would sprout into rebellion against the Creator.

Once he established the "unfair" limits God had placed on human freedom, it was easy for the serpent to point out the benefits of disregarding such unreasonable restrictions. "'You will not surely die,' the serpent said to the woman. 'For God knows that when you eat of it your eyes will be opened, and you will be like God, knowing good and evil'" (Gen. 3:4-5).

The temptation worked. "When the woman saw that the fruit of the tree was good for food and pleasing to the eye, and also desirable for gaining wisdom, she took some and ate it. She also gave some to her husband, who was with her, and he ate it" (Gen. 3:6). They did with the tree the one thing—the only thing—they had been forbidden to do: they used its fruit for food to satisfy their cravings and their curiosity.

The results were disastrous both for human beings and for the land.

"'Cursed is the ground because of you; through painful toil you will eat of it all the days of your life. It will produce thorns and thistles for you, and you will eat the plants of the field'" (Gen. 3:17-18). The natural world over which we had been given dominion was carried down with us when we fell.

How can we describe Adam's grief when the animals he had named fled from him? When the ground from which he had sprung, which he had tended for God, yielded thorns instead of fruit?

Whose fault?

God changed the first humans' relationship with nature, but only because they had changed it first. The tragedy developed because Adam and Eve asserted their independence and took creation into their own hands. They had been placed in the garden to serve and watch over it in a caring way that would preserve it for its true owner. Now they had arrogantly placed themselves in the role of using the natural world to get what they wanted. "Their disobedience brought discord and alienation into God's good creation. This alienation intruded into every human relationship—between humans and God, among humans, and between humans and the rest of creation" (Wright, *Biology Through the Eyes of Faith,* p. 171).

> The fall disrupted not only humanity's relation to God, but also its relationship to God's creation. Construing dominion to mean having all power over creation reflects the desire to be "like God" and the central fact of sin and the fall. Sin began, after all, with humanity deciding to ignore God and do what it pleased with God's creation. (Granberg-Michaelson, "At the Dawn of the New Creation," *Sojourners*)

We are the heirs of the first misuse of dominion over the earth, the first trespass from the role of creature into the role of creator. "Sin entered the world through one man, and death through sin, and in this way death came to all men, because all sinned" (Rom. 5:12).

Imperfect obedience

Since the Fall, even humanity's best efforts to obey the command to "have dominion" have been imperfect, and at worst we have flagrantly disobeyed it. That means that ever since Eden, the com-

108

mand to subdue the earth *has never been fulfilled in the way that God originally meant it.* The fault, then, is not in the command to have dominion. It is the misguided carrying out—and the willful ignoring—of the command to have dominion that brings devastation to the created earth.

In short, we have another example of the old problem of confusing—and we all do it—the ideal toward which we strive and the faltering, pathetically imperfect level of actual performance. . . . However, the misuse of a God-given gift by the recipient does not in itself condemn either the gift or the giver. (Bullock, "Coming Catastrophes," *Journal of American Scientific Association*)

What are the ecological implications of the doctrine of the fall of humanity?

The first will sound negative at first. As things are now, before Christ returns, *the earth cannot be restored to Eden.* That's true for two reasons: humanity continues to be imperfect, and the natural order is damaged.

Ecologists call for a sustainable system of agriculture, productivity, and manufacturing—all renewing itself and keeping itself going in harmony and balance. Yet it's worth asking whether "sustainability" is even achievable in a fallen world.

Behind our Western discussion of ecology and natural order lies a massive assumption: Life as it is on the Earth is good and so must be preserved. But what if life is not good, but brutish and mean? Balance is easy for us to endorse after a good dinner in a heated building, but what does it mean to the woman hauling fifty pounds of wood several hours a day [to cook for her family]?

The problem with our search for stability of the ecosystem is that *something has gone dreadfully wrong with the system.* It is sick unto death, a sickness that is narrated in the early chapters of

Genesis. (Dyrness, "Are We Our Planet's Keeper?" *Christianity Today*, emphasis added)

That's the bad news. The good news is that *the story of the fall does not end with humanity's loss and a curse on the ground.*

God is righteous; he is also merciful. He first clothed Adam and Eve with "garments of skin" before expelling them from the Garden, lest they "take also from the tree of life and eat, and live forever" (Gen. 3:21-22). God did not abandon the earth and in particular he did not abandon the flawed, wandering human creatures who had made such a wreck of their privileged position.

Throughout the Bible we can see evidence of the value God places on his fallen creation. There are prophets and miracles and rescues on every page. The best evidence of God's estimate of his creation is that God himself entered that creation as one of those weak human creatures, subject to our human limitations, but without the fatal flaw.

In the life and death of Christ, God took on himself the sour fruit of the ruin of creation. He was *incarnate:* God "with us," God *in the flesh.* Because we live as physical creatures of flesh and blood, Jesus shared our humanity by taking on the same kind of body we have. It was a gnostic heresy that Jesus had no physical body and only appeared to suffer and die. In his body he endured the limitations of time and space, subject to weariness and temptations and even, ultimately, to death, so that he "might taste death for everyone" (Heb. 2:9).

But Jesus' death was no tragic victimization. His death destroyed the power of death over us, overcoming the Fall, paying for our sins, redeeming the broken world. He was made like us "in every way, in order that he might become a merciful and faithful high priest in service to God, and that he might make atonement for the sins of the people" (Heb. 2:14–17).

The Extent of Redemption

"God so loved the *world* that he gave his one and only Son, that whoever believes in him shall not perish but have eternal life" (John 3:16, emphasis added). The word *world* is *kosmos* and it usually has the negative connotations of "the world's system," the sin-flawed way things are run "down here."

Evangelical Christians are very familiar with all of this. The question that relates to ecology is: Precisely *what* was redeemed in the death and resurrection of Christ? Are we only saved individually and spiritually out of this sinful milieu, or does Christ's salvation have some universal effect on all of creation just as human sin affected it?

Here we must differentiate between sin and sins. Creation today is not what God originally meant it to be. When *sin* entered the world, somehow it took the created world down with it, and the earth is still waiting to be remade at the coming of Christ. Humankind's continuing *sins* have damaged the earth through wasteful and greedy practices. Though the effects of sin on nature cannot yet be reversed (for they affected the very "nature of nature"), the effects of sins can be repaired to some extent, and further sins can be refrained from.

That the redemption God provides is both present and future is evident from Romans 8. First we have the assurance that the power of sin *has already* been broken:

Therefore, there is now no condemnation for those who are in Christ Jesus, because through Christ Jesus the law of the Spirit of life set me free from the law of sin and death. For what the law was powerless to do in that it was weakened by the sinful nature, God did by sending his own Son in the likeness of sinful man to be a sin offering. (Rom. 8:1-3)

111

Then Paul gives us the tantalizing idea that where creation was entangled with humanity's fall, it is also involved with humanity's redemption:

> I consider that our present sufferings are not worth comparing with the glory that will be revealed in us. The creation waits in eager expectation for the sons of God to be revealed. For the creation was subjected to frustration, not by its own choice, but by the will of the one who subjected it, in hope that the creation itself will be liberated from its bondage to decay and brought into the glorious freedom of the children of God.
>
> We know that the whole creation has been groaning as in the pains of childbirth right up to the present time. Not only so, but we ourselves, who have the firstfruits of the Spirit, groan inwardly as we wait eagerly for our adoption as sons, the redemption of our bodies. (Rom. 8:18-23)

At an Au Sable Forum in 1984, Bishop Paulos Gregorios of Delhi, India, offered this translation of Romans 8:19: "The whole creation stands on tippy-toes, with neck outstretched . . . awaiting the redemption of the children of God." J.B. Phillips paraphrased it: "The whole creation is on tiptoe to see the wonderful sight of the sons of God coming into their own."

All through chapters 5 through 7 of Romans, Paul struggles with the question of the completeness of our redemption and the fact that we still deal with sin in our present lives. His message is that although sin is at work in us, and although the victory is not complete until Christ returns, we can have *substantial* victory over it now. That is also the message for God's creation, over which (though it is flawed and we are flawed) we are still entrusted with dominion.

Over twenty years ago Francis Schaeffer wrote an important work on ecology, *Pollution and the Death of Man.* He had this to say about the tension between the "now" and "not yet" of earth's redemption: "Christians who believe the Bible are not simply called to say that 'one day' there will be healing, but that by God's grace *substantially,* upon the basis of the work of Christ, *substantial healing* can be a reality here and now" (Schaeffer, *Pollution and the Death of Man,* p. 67, emphasis added).

In the same way in which we look for substantial healing in all our relationships, we are to look for substantial healing in creation. Just as we work to achieve reconciliation in all our relationships, our work includes reconciliation with the creation.

We don't need to be trained theologians to realize that the redemption from sin is not yet complete on this earth *in all its effects.* We would be naive to think so. Sin and its consequences can be seen everywhere, and they will not be eradicated completely until Christ returns. But in the meantime, the effects of the redemption of Jesus can also be seen everywhere, if we look for them. By faith we enter into his redemption and participate in his work of redeeming what has been lost.

How do we start? Not by legislation or by coercing others to conform to our views. We start with recognition that we are fallen, we accept the redemption of Christ, and we begin the revision of our own values. That's the theme of the next chapter.

CHAPTER NINE

THE GOD-CENTERED VALUES OF WORSHIP AND TRUST

O Almighty and everlasting God,
who hast graciously given unto us the fruits of the earth in their season;
We yield thee humble and hearty thanks for this thy bounty;
beseeching thee to give us grace rightly to use the same to thy glory,
and the relief of those that need; through Jesus Christ our Lord,
who liveth and reigneth with thee and the Holy Ghost,
one God, world without end. Amen.
Collect for A Form of Thanksgiving for the Blessings of Harvest,
Church of Ireland Book of Common Prayer, 1549

These days we don't often have the chance to witness the mushrooming of an old-fashioned "boom town."

Doing the circle tour around Lake Superior a couple of summers ago, we were driving through Ontario on the northernmost side of the lake. We were going west to east, which means for mile after mile we had the black-rock lakeshore to the right, the forest stretching away northward to the left. Towns, few and far between, were picturesque and quiet.

Then we came to Marathon, where the recent discovery of gold is producing an economic boom.

Gold Rush

In Marathon, brand-new houses lined dirt streets cut hurriedly into the earth. Unpaved parking lots and piles of dirt shoved here and there surrounded shiny new mini-malls and video stores and gas stations. The effect was a breathless rush to cash in on the new money. It was not attractive.

Marathon residents, if they read this, would probably answer that unemployment is not so pretty either. Because they depend so heavily on shipping, lumbering, mining, and tourism, all communities on Lake Superior—including ours—get hit hard by economic slumps. Who wouldn't want to cash in on the gold rush?

What's best for Marathon and environs? We could argue about it for weeks. From a secular point of view, it would come down to weighing economic values versus environmental values: which should be protected—the environment or the economy? (Interestingly, the words *economy* and *ecology* come from the same root: *oikos,* Greek for "house." Economy is the managing of the house; ecology is how the whole house fits together.) The discussion would come down to my ideas vs. your ideas, my vision of the ideal world vs. yours.

We've seen how both the human-centered and the earth-centered views of nature are bent on attaining and preserving a particular lifestyle. That effort, understandable as it is, can never be a sufficient motive for *Christians* to make ecological judgments.

Then do Christians have anything unique to say about a place like Marathon, Ontario? Or any other spot on earth where economic development and natural qualities seem to be at war? Of course we do. But what we say won't necessarily be what somebody else thinks is politically correct. We offer another, different, refreshing third alternative. It has its own costs and its own rewards.

It's all too easy to let ourselves be intimidated by secular environmentalists, stammering and apologizing for how little and late has been the church's response to the problem. Maybe it has been little and late; but once we *have* thought through the issues, we do not need to apologize for expressing a uniquely Christian viewpoint on ecology. We can say it in a voice that neither parrots whatever is in vogue *nor* hides its head in the sand pretending there's no problem.

What gives us the right to speak out? What gives us the content of what to say? Our authority must be something more basic than the fact that we favor or don't favor a particular political system, or that we happen to like or dislike a particular way of looking at nature.

Happy or thankful?

Last Thanksgiving, a local day-care center published a list of things the preschoolers were thankful for . . . sort of. Since (the ad explained) "thankful" was too abstract a concept for these little ones to grasp, they were asked instead, "What makes you *happy*?"

The children answered with things like "My blanket," "My Teddy bear," and (surely gratifying to some parents) "Mommy" and "Daddy." They were nice answers, clearly spontaneous and from the kids' hearts. But why in the world do parents teach, prompt, and drill young children to say "Thank you" if all it means is, "I'm happy"?

There is all the difference in the world between being "thankful" and being "happy." To be "happy" is to experience a good feeling totally within the person who is lucky enough to feel that way. To be "thankful" is to express gratitude to *another* person who has done something for us, something generous and undeserved.

The day-care center's ad is unconsciously profound; it demonstrates our fatal ecological flaw. As we live with the riches of God's creation, we do not know the difference between being happy and being thankful. No matter whether we eat up earth's resources or observe its splendor without consuming it, if we only let nature "make us happy," then we forget there is a Person to be thanked for it all.

A uniquely Christian ecology begins with that Person. A Christian ecological response is the living out of gratitude to the Person who made this world and who (amazingly) still entrusts it to our fallible care.

117

Unique Voice, Unique Hope

A genuine Christian ecology begins not with our relationship to the earth—important as that is—but with our relationship to a personal God. And it is absolutely vital to say that he *is* a Person, not a "Force" (shoving ahead of itself all things good and bad) or "The All" (you, me, the trees, the nuclear waste dumps, the cancer cells) or "Divinity" (a shapeless mound of sweet white stuff).

That Person is precisely what (or *who*) is missing in both the technological and the mystical views of ecology. We've seen how both those views wind up human-centered, and as Father Vincent Rossi puts it, the Christian answer to "anthropocentrism" is not "biocentrism" but "theocentrism." The way to combat the destructiveness of putting humanity at the center of the universe is not to dethrone humanity and enthrone "the biosphere" in our place; rather it is to acknowledge that God is on the throne, at the center, and has been all along (Rossi, "Theocentrism," *Epiphany Journal*).

Here is the unique voice and the unique hope offered by Christianity. Christians' reference point is a holy God who is *other than* the created order—a perfectly objective, perfectly wise third party who stands outside the discussion, so to speak—yet who is also *here*, who has entered creation dramatically, authoritatively, redemptively, in Jesus Christ.

That is a fine theory, but what would a God-centered ecology *look like?* More specifically, what will people do if they have a God-centered view of living on this earth?

Two dangerous words

A God-centered ecology will reflect *worship* of God and *trust* in God.

Now those are dangerous words to use, because much contemporary religious experience interprets "worship" and "trust" as subjective feelings. I go to church and feel high from singing the

118

praise songs, and I call that sensation "worship." I assume that good fortune will come to me if I have faith, and I call that confidence "trust."

Worship and trust are not inner-directed feelings; they are other-directed *attitudes*—specifically, attitudes toward God. They might produce subjective feelings; they certainly produce external actions. Worship and trust in God make a difference in what people *do* to each other and to God's earth and the creatures that live on it.

"Worship" literally means showing honor because of the *worth* of another. Because we worship the One of ultimate worth, God the Creator, we care for the world he has made, not simply for its own sake but because *he whom we love and worship* has made it.

"Trust" is relying on another, as opposed to relying on ourselves or circumstances or fate or some clever scheme or device. Because we trust God the Provider, we don't need to feel driven to drain the last drop from earth's resources. The One we trust will provide for us.

Though we speak of being "awed" at a mountain range or the expanse of the ocean, it is not this earth that Christians worship, beautiful as it is. We worship the Creator of the earth, the Redeemer who became a man and lived and died here, the Spirit who is present in the world.

> The earth with its store of wonders untold,
> Almighty, thy power hath founded of old,
> Hath stablished it fast by a changeless decree,
> And round it hath cast, like a mantle, the sea.
> ("O Worship The King," Robert H. Grant, 1833, v. 3)

"Small enough"

The story is told that Franklin D. Roosevelt and his friend Bernard Baruch talked late into the night one evening at the White House. At last President Roosevelt suggested they go out into the Rose Garden and look at the stars before going to bed. They went out and looked up for several minutes, peering up toward the thousands of points of light above. Then the President said, "All right, I think we feel small enough now to go in and go to sleep."

Contemplating God's creation does make us feel small. It made David ask:

When I consider your heavens,
  the work of your fingers,
the moon and the stars,
  which you have set in place,
what is man that you are mindful of him,
  the son of man that you care for him? (Ps. 8:3-4)

The sense of our insignificance is not the end of the story. Our worship does not have to remain "from afar." Because Jesus is our high priest who became a man, we can "approach the throne of grace with confidence, so that we may receive mercy and find grace to help us in our time of need" (Heb. 4:16).

In his generosity God lets us draw near to him, to walk with him like Enoch (Gen. 5:24), to talk with him as a friend like Moses (Exod. 33:11), to be his friend like Abraham (Isa. 41:8; James 2:23). We are invited to live "in the shelter of the Most High" and to "rest in the shadow of the Almighty" (Ps. 91:1). Along with John we can rest our head on him (John 13:23) and come to know the power of "Christ in you, the hope of glory" (Col. 1:27). Above all we can join the company in heaven singing: "'Worthy is the Lamb, who was slain, to receive power and wealth and wisdom and strength and honor and glory and praise!'" (Rev. 5:12).

A faith that loses such intimacy with God is going to turn up empty. Its only validation will be in the form of rituals or the accumulation of gifts in response to its prayers—and even these will eventually become empty.

In a recent letter to Ann Landers, a grandmother wrote lamenting that her grandchildren were complaining because they hadn't received their birthday gifts yet. Somehow the gifts, meant to be expressions of a special relationship, had become rights to be demanded from an impersonal provider.

Like children ripping open our presents under the Christmas tree, we get so caught up in all God's gifts that we forget the Giver. If we neglect our worship of the Lord, we will be back to Adam Smith's view of people relating to things in purely economic transactions, rather than people relating to people as creations of God.

Without God or good personal relationships, what can we do but turn to worshiping material things for all our meaning? Our "worship" is then crassly materialistic whether we worship commodities or natural phenomena. Either way, as in the Bible, people "worshiped and served created things rather than the Creator" (Rom. 1:25).

Faith Doesn't Panic

Have you noticed that most environmental material has an element of panic about it? We must save the earth *or else*. Saving this earth is our only hope.

Christians have much better reasons than alarm and panic for being concerned for the natural world. Our trust is not in this earth being saved; our trust is not in this earth at all; it is in God. We believe in a living Creator, a Redeemer who became a man, and a Spirit who is present in the world. We have the revealed Scripture by which to evaluate all ideas. Our faith gives us a refreshing alternative to the nervous self-protection of both secular environmentalists and exploiters of the earth.

Jesus' message—and his life—was one of faith, trusting in a caring heavenly Father.

Therefore I tell you, do not worry about your life, what you will eat or drink; or about your body, what you will wear. Is not life more important than food, and the body more important than clothes? Look at the birds of the air; they do not sow or reap or store away in barns, and yet your heavenly Father feeds them. Are you not much more valuable than they? (Matt. 6:25-27)

Sin entered the world through a lack of faith. Not fully trusting God, Adam and Eve ate of the fruit of the knowledge of good and evil, hoping to gain what God had withheld from them. "They had decided not to believe God. That is the real issue. It's true that disobedience is the immediate cause of the fall, but prior to disobedience is unbelief, or loss of faith—a ceasing to rely on God and his trustworthiness" (Alexander, "Tragedy & Hope in Genesis 3," *Spiritual Counterfeits Project Journal*).

Like Adam and Eve, we have a tendency to leave God out of the equation as we make our daily decisions. We may still worship God, but "worship" gets confined to a couple of hours a week in a church service. We may say a perfunctory grace before meals (have you ever stopped eating and wondered if you've said grace yet?).

That's far from the outlook of the psalmist who wrote:

I will exalt you, my God the King;
    I will praise your name for ever and ever.
Every day I will praise you
    and extol your name for ever and ever.
Great is the LORD and most worthy of praise;
    his greatness no one can fathom.
One generation will commend your works to another;
    they will tell of your mighty acts.
They will speak of the glorious splendor of your majesty,
    and I will meditate on your wonderful works.
They will tell of the power of your awesome works,
    and I will proclaim your great deeds.
They will celebrate your abundant goodness
    and joyfully sing of your righteousness.
The LORD is gracious and compassionate,
    slow to anger and rich in love.

The LORD is good to all;
>   he has compassion on all he has made.
All you have made will praise you, O LORD;
>   your saints will extol you. (Ps. 145:1-10)

The psalm writer's worship and trust are constant and a natural part of life. Here is a celebration of God himself, his character, his greatness and goodness, and especially his compassion. For this writer, worship and trust are simply a way of life, an expression of consistent faith in God.

Living it out

How will worship and trust *look* in everyday life? How will we see them making a difference in the way we conduct ourselves and how we treat the natural world?

In the first place, they will keep us mindful of God's presence on this earth. We will remember that he has not gone on vacation; he is right here—not like a prison guard watching our every move, but a loving presence who never overlooks or forgets us.

As guests in the home of gracious friends, we may enjoy a generous meal, but the food is not our main interest; we are more interested in nurturing a warm relationship. The last thing we want to do is to abuse their china or their rugs. Their stuff is *theirs,* not ours, and we treat it well out of our regard for them, not merely because it is nice stuff.

Likewise, loving God and living on his earth, we will treat kindly the things God has made. Francis Schaeffer wrote of the difference it makes when we "love the Lover":

If individually and in the Christian community I treat with integrity the things God has made, and treat them this way lovingly, because they are His, things change. If I love the Lover, I love what the Lover has made. Perhaps this is the reason so many

123

Christians feel an unreality in their Christian lives. If I don't love what the Lover has made—in the area of man, in the area of nature—and really love it because He made it, do I really love the Lover at all? (Schaeffer, *Pollution and the Death of Man,* pp. 91-92)

If we worship God, we will not abuse the things he has made, and if we trust God—and this is a hard lesson for all of us—we'll know it is *not* entirely up to us to provide security for ourselves. That's a liberating idea and, though it can be taken as an excuse for laziness, it will set us free from *having* to accumulate everything we think we need or will ever need.

Christians who are truly trusting God are not compelled to be big consumers, users, throwers-away. From prison Paul wrote, "I know what it is to be in need, and I know what it is to have plenty. I have learned the secret of being content in any and every situation, whether well fed or hungry, whether living in plenty or in want. . . . And my God will meet all your needs according to his glorious riches in Christ Jesus" (Phil. 4:12, 19). The psalmist expressed his rest in God's loving care: "I lie down and sleep; I wake again, because the LORD sustains me" (Ps. 3:5). "You are my Lord; apart from you I have no good thing" (Ps. 16:2).

Must we scheme to find some way to get the latest? Must we even *have* the latest? Not if we are trusting the Lord to give us what we need. Not if God is our joy and our sufficiency.

The Land of Forgetfulness?

When Israel was on the way to the land of promise, God promised them prosperity, yet he knew prosperity could tempt them to take credit for it themselves and forget him.

When the LORD your God brings you into the land he swore to your fathers, to Abraham, Isaac and Jacob, to give you—a land with large flourishing cities you did not build, houses filled with all kinds of good things you did not provide, wells you did not dig, and vineyards and olive groves you did not plant—then when you eat and are satisfied, be careful that you do not forget the LORD, who brought you out of Egypt, out of the land of slavery. (Deut. 6:10-12)

God's words came true. As Israel trusted God, they prospered and grew powerful. In their prosperity they kept drifting away from God until he brought judgment and deliverance.

John Wesley, founder of Methodism, feared that the same forgetfulness would plague Christians:

I fear that wherever riches have increased, the essence of religion has decreased in the same proportion. Therefore, I do not see how it is possible, in the nature of things, for any revival of true religion to continue long. For religion must of necessity produce both industry and frugality, and these cannot but produce riches. But as riches increase, so will pride, anger, and love of the world in all its branches. (John Wesley, quoted by David E. Shi in *In Search of the Simple Life,* p. 30)

True repentance begins to renew our relationship with God completely apart from his gifts.

First we must admit that our values have been wrong. For some of us it may take an end to being "happy" in order to become "thankful." Then and only then will we know the difference. Some of us must lose what we have in order to understand that it was all on loan from God. As long as we consider the things we have (and getting more) as our "rights," we will have no time or room for worshiping and trusting the Giver.

The last psalm has thirteen lines. Only one does not begin with "praise," and that one *ends* with "praise"! Yet not a single word is said in Psalm 150 about the gifts of God. It is all pure praise to God.

One way of renewing our relationship with God is to take time, to make time if necessary, to join the psalmist, looking at the sky and the other works of God that "declare the glory of God" and "proclaim the work of his hands" (Ps. 19:1). One of the ironies of working on this book for the past few months is that there have been many beautiful days when we were cooped up inside, too busy writing *about* nature to *enjoy* nature. We know other naturalists who are frustrated by the "desk job" aspects of their work. For most of us it takes effort to give ourselves the chance to see and touch God's creation.

Often we keep ourselves so insulated by our own "works" that there is little room for wonder at the works of One far greater than ourselves. We may need to cut ourselves off deliberately from our own gadgets and spend time in nature apart from the things we have made for ourselves. Then we give God a chance to ask us what he asked Job: "Where were you when I laid the earth's foundation? . . . Can you bind the beautiful Pleiades? Can you loose the cords of Orion? Can you bring forth the constellations in their seasons or lead out the Bear with its cubs?" (Job 38:4, 31-32).

A nation of shoppers

In *The End of Nature,* Bill McKibben puts forth an interesting choice: "Should we so choose, we could exercise our reason to do what no other animal can do: we could limit ourselves voluntarily, choose to remain God's creatures instead of making ourselves gods." He suggests that God has "granted us free will and now looks on, with great concern and love, to see how we exercise it: to see if we take the chance offered by this crisis to bow down and humble ourselves, or if we compound original sin with terminal sin" (McKibben, *The End of Nature,* pp. 214, 216).

"Limit ourselves"? "Humble ourselves"? Who wants to hear about that? We don't want to cut back on what we have; we would prefer to keep what we have, thank you, and add to it while we're at it. America did not become a nation of shopping malls because its people had a passion for self-denial. Even as we think of ways to solve our environmental problems, "Our impulse will be to adapt not ourselves but the earth. We will . . . try to figure out a new way to continue our domination, and hence our accustomed life-style" (ibid., 150).

It is that domination of life, that clinging to what we can get, from which true Christian faith liberates us. Worship and trust in the Creator as revealed in Jesus Christ is the best hope for ecology.

Faithful discretion

Our unique approach sets us apart from other environmental activists even while we join with them in some efforts. As Christians we will agree with causes that fit our world view; we will give thoughtful critique of the rest. We are not bound to accept anyone else's views of what must be done or when it must be done.

Along the way we may join with some secular environmental efforts, but we will have our own uniquely Christian reasons for doing so. Sometimes our alignments will surprise outsiders, but we will have our own reasons for supporting some endeavors and distancing ourselves from others. We may have to part company with some movements along the way and join others or form our own because of our higher loyalty to God.

Next we want to look more specifically at how worship and trust in the Lord will affect two areas: caring for land and living with justice.

CHAPTER TEN
CARING FOR LAND

We get the earth for nothing, don't we?
It's given to us, gift on gift:
Sun on the floor, airs in the curtain.
We lie a whole day long and look at it
Crowing or crying in our cribs:
It doesn't matter—crow or cry
The sun shines, the wind blows.
Archibald MacLeish, **J.B.**

The generation of Israelites who finally entered Canaan had known only a nomadic herding life. During their time in the desert, God gave them laws that presumed a settled society of farms and villages. He was preparing them for "when the LORD your God brings you into the land which he swore to your fathers, to Abraham, Isaac, and Jacob, to give you" (Deut. 6:10).

God never lays down law for the sake of law; his laws come from his love. They always show a sense of compassion for their subjects and objects. God makes laws because he cares about the people and things those laws touch. The laws he gave in the desert about mundane details of agriculture—sowing, harvesting, handling animals, sharing the harvest with others—are not there just to have some "farm laws" on the books. They are there because God cares that farming, like everything else, will be done with respect toward everyone and everything involved.

Laws for the Land

The Israelites were about to meet up with the "natives" who had their own concepts of how deity relates to land. The Canaanites lived in the service—and the fear—of gods of the earth and its seasons. They practiced fertility rites to placate their deities and insure the growth of crops and the increase of flocks and herds. Baal, the "dying and rising god" whose worship would continue to tantalize the Israelites, was imagined doing battle with the forces of chaos. He would temporarily lose as vegetation withered and died, but would rise again with its new growth.

The Israelites were warned again and again not to try to appease the earth-gods of Canaan. With that kind of earth-idolatry threatening all around, we might expect God's law carefully to avoid personifying the land or regarding it as something that can be treated well or abused.

Instead we find the fields and pastures surprisingly prominent in the laws God gave the Israelites. He had plenty to say about the land on which they would soon raise crops and graze their herds.

God promised them that the land he was providing was not miserly but good and fruitful. Clearly it is a good thing to God that land produces well and sufficiently provides for the people who live on it.

For the LORD your God is bringing you into a good land—a land with streams and pools of water, with springs flowing in the valleys and hills; a land with wheat and barley, vines and fig trees, pomegranates, olive oil and honey; a land where bread will not be scarce and you will lack nothing; a land where the rocks are iron and you can dig copper out of the hills. . . . a land flowing with milk and honey. The land you are entering to take over is not like

130

the land of Egypt, from which you have come, where you planted your seed and irrigated it by foot as in a vegetable garden. But the land you are crossing the Jordan to take possession of is a land of mountains and valleys that drinks rain from heaven. It is a land the LORD your God cares for; the eyes of the LORD your God are continually on it from the beginning of the year to its end. (Deut. 8:7-9, 11:9b-12)

The Lord tied the productivity of Canaan directly to Israel's obedience to him (Deut. 11:12-17). The obedience-fruitfulness connection was not magic ("do these rituals and God will make the wheat grow")—*that* was the essence of the Canaanite fertility religion. The obedience God called for would be expressed in the way the Israelites treated each other and the land God gave them.

A sabbath for land

As the people looked forward to a "land flowing with milk and honey" they must have wondered at one particular law: the sabbath year. As the law provided for a day of rest every seventh day for people and animals (Deut. 5:12-14), so the land was to receive a year of rest every seven years.

The LORD said to Moses on Mount Sinai, "Speak to the Israelites and say to them: 'When you enter the land I am going to give you, the land itself must observe a sabbath to the LORD. For six years sow your fields, and for six years prune your vineyards and gather their crops. But in the seventh year the land is to have a sabbath of rest, a sabbath to the LORD. Do not sow your field or prune your vineyards. Do not reap what grows of itself or harvest the grapes of your untended vines. The land is to have a year of rest. (Lev. 25:1-5)

At least two things are implied in the sabbath year: recognition of Israel's need for faith and respect for the needs of the land.

The sabbath year reminded people *whose* land they really lived on—and that he could be trusted. It was a sabbath "to the Lord." To obey this law the people would have to trust God to provide for them for *three* uncertain years: the seventh while they refrained from planting their fields, the eighth when they could finally plant, and the ninth when the plantings of the eighth would be harvested.

There would be temptations:

- The temptation to hoard as though God wouldn't be there next year.
- The temptation to plant and harvest anyway because "I have special circumstances."
- The temptation to worry, to count every grain of wheat and calculate their chances of survival on human terms.
- The temptation to stop sharing and stop tithing because they might not have "enough."

Jesus' words centuries later in the Sermon on the Mount would have spoken to those early Israelites as well: "So do not worry, saying, 'What shall we eat?' or 'What shall we drink?' or 'What shall we wear?' For the pagans run after all these things, and your heavenly Father knows that you need them. But seek first his kingdom and his righteousness, and all these things will be given to you as well" (Matt. 6:31-33). They didn't have the Sermon on the Mount, but they had God's promise through Moses:

I will send you such a blessing in the sixth year that the land will yield enough for three years. While you plant during the eighth year, you will eat from the old crop and will continue to eat from it until the harvest of the ninth year comes in. (Lev. 25:21-22)

The law of the sabbath year was good for more than the people. It was good for the land. God cared that the physical earth would be treated with respect and not be abused. The people were not simply to take all they could get from the land; they must allow it time to renew itself. It's a principle of good farming that farmland needs to lie fallow occasionally. If it is farmed continuously with no chance to rejuvenate, it will be exhausted and turn into a dust bowl.

Jubilee!

Along with a "rest" for the land every seventh year, God ordered a special "release" every fifty years.

Jubilee is a word applied to everything from a sale at the local grocery store to the title of Prison Fellowship's newsletter. "This is the year of jubilee!" sang slaves released after the Civil War. In the Old Testament the "Year of Jubilee" *was* something to sing about—a cause for rejoicing all over the land.

In the law of the Year of Jubilee, God set forth a principle that undercuts any illusions that land is "mine, all mine." The principle was this: "The land must not be sold permanently, because the land is mine and you are but aliens and my tenants" (Lev. 25:23). The earth belongs to God, not to people. God's law put automatic constraints on the accumulation of land, particularly at others' expense.

"Proclaim liberty throughout all the land" says the inscription on the Liberty Bell—a direct quote from God's law of Jubilee. In the fiftieth year, on the Day of Atonement, trumpets would sound and liberty would be proclaimed. What kind of liberty? The liberty of being able to return to one's homeland regardless of who had taken possession of it in the meantime. "It shall be a jubilee for you; each one of you is to return to his family property and each to his own clan. . . . In this Year of Jubilee everyone is to return to his own property" (Lev. 25:10, 13).

We can overhear the more land-wealthy Israelites' thoughts as the 50th year approached:

- "I'm losing everything I've accumulated for 49 years!"
- "What will I leave for my children?"
- "Those people didn't do anything to earn this!"

But it was God's way of keeping land use equitable. By law, families' land rights could not be violated or canceled, not even by debt. Each family was allotted a parcel of land that stayed in the family. If they became too poor to support themselves, they were allowed to exchange the land for a period of time. If possible, a relative could redeem it for them. But even if no one redeemed it, it reverted to the original owner at the Year of Jubilee (Lev. 25:25-28).

Notice that it was not against the law to accumulate land. The wealthy could buy more land as they were able. But the Year of Jubilee put limits on the extension of their land holdings. They could not be rich forever at the expense of the poor. They could not lay claim to the land *forever.*

The people were to keep the Jubilee in mind as they bought and sold. It was a constant constraint on the temptation to take advantage of one another. "You are to buy from your countryman on the basis of the number of years since the Jubilee. And he is to sell to you on the basis of the number of years left for harvesting crops" (Lev. 25:15).

God's laws are not arbitrary legalities. In the law we see "new values" lived out in the way the Israelites were to conduct themselves in the new land.

> Throughout the Jewish scriptures the land is God's, not a commodity to be owned by human beings. All the creatures are seen as praising God. In Jesus' teaching God cares for the sparrows and for the lilies of the field. Jesus taught that God cares even more for human beings, but the care for the lilies and for the sparrows is not just for the sake of human beings; it is for the lilies and the sparrows themselves. (Daly and Cobb, *For the Common Good,* p. 385)

It's reasonable to be curious about how the nomadic Israelites really did treat the land once they finally got there and began to be settled farmers. Fortunately archaeology lets us satisfy at least some of our curiosity.

134

Historical insight

The book of Joshua tells us that when the Israelites entered Canaan, they made short work of overcoming the cities of Jericho and Ai. They spread throughout Canaan conquering other cities and taking possession as the land had been designated by lot to their family groups (Josh. 14:1-5). But their "conquest" became less and less aggressive. They found it was more comfortable to coexist with the Canaanites, so that Joshua had to ask, "How long will you wait before you begin to take possession of the land that the LORD, the God of your fathers, has given you?" (Josh. 18:3).

Small, non-fortified Israelite villages appeared on hilltops among the fortified Canaanite cities. They began to make the transition to agriculture, but they were crowded with the pressure of the still-remaining Canaanite population.

When Ephraim and Manasseh complained that they did not have enough land, Joshua told them to go into the forested hills and clear ground for themselves. They replied that the hill country was not enough, but they could not dispossess the Canaanites in the lowlands because they had iron chariots. Joshua encouraged them to go ahead and clear the hill country.

That may sound like ecologically unsound advice from Joshua. But archaeology has revealed how the emerging Israelite farmers handled their new territory.

Once the forests were cleared, the Israelites created agricultural terraces on the land. . . . Terracing transformed the natural slopes into series of level steps—artificially flattened surfaces or "fields"—suitable for farming. Terrace soils were anchored in place by retaining walls built of dry-laid stones. The terrace walls, which were usually built on the natural contours at right angles to the slope, countered soil erosion and, to a lesser degree, induced sedimentation. (Stager, "The Song of Deborah," *Biblical Archaeology Review*)

Evidence of those terraces can still be seen on the Judean hillsides, dated to the times that Israelite tribes settled there. Unfortunately the terraces eventually deteriorated without regular maintenance, but they were an attempt at sustainable agriculture under pressured conditions when the fertile lowlands were not available. Stager believes that the "high places" belonging to Naphtali (Judg. 5:18, KJV) actually refer to such terraced fields.

We do not know whether Israel ever actually observed the Year of Jubilee; archaeology and history do not tell us. Maybe they looked at it as good theory, but bad business.

And maybe at this point history is looking irrelevant. We may have no more "land" than a backyard full of dandelions—if that. We don't live in Canaan and most of us are in situations very unlike the early Israelites. Do God's laws still speak to us about how to treat whatever "land" comes under our care?

Do the Laws Make Any Difference?

The history of agriculture shows us what happens when the simple rules of Leviticus and Deuteronomy are ignored.

C. Dean Freudenberger, professor of Christian ethics at Claremont School of Theology, has been a consultant on soil and agriculture in more than thirty countries over a period of thirty-five years. His book *Global Dust Bowl* gives us a good idea of what happens when God's principles for land use are—and are not—followed.

In his chapter "A Brief History of Agriculture," Freudenberger tells how nation after nation has "changed and often destroyed the land." He goes on to say, "During the Roman conquests, the 'grain belt' of North Africa gave way to deserts, to dust bowls. . . . The Romans loved their native soil and called it *mater terra,* 'mother earth.' But whether the earth provided for other people in other nations was no concern of theirs." The land of other nations was simply used to feed and increase the wealth of Rome.

136

In the 1600s, Western European colonial agriculture came to the North American continent. In the southern colonies this meant growing tobacco (and later cotton) for export. The Danes occupied the Caribbean Islands and produced sugar there. Slaves were imported for both the Caribbean and southern plantations. The "golden triangle" of American trade included rum, guns, and slaves. Agriculture in North America as in the (former) Belgian Congo, was organized to "bring another land area into the economy of western Europe." (Freudenberger, *Global Dust Bowl,* pp. 70-74)

Land use was no longer to clothe and feed the people who lived there; it was only to bring wealth and prosperity to those who controlled it. Once the laws of God are discounted, what reason is there *not* to use the land this way?

With such a world view, the lands of the "New World" had value only as they could be turned into wealth by producing consumer goods. Ironically, that idolatrous view of land eventually produces a disregard, even a disdain, for the goods the land produces. That's why so much of our land is given over to garbage dumps.

Abuse and loss

During his 1960 trek over America in his truck, John Steinbeck noticed one way that American cities resemble each other.

American cities are like badger holes, ringed with trash—all of them—surrounded by piles of wrecked and rusting automobiles, and almost smothered with rubbish. . . . I do wonder whether there will come a time when we can no longer afford our wastefulness—chemical wastes in the rivers, metal wastes everywhere, and atomic wastes buried deep in the earth or sunk in the sea. When an Indian village became too deep in its own filth, the inhabitants moved. And we have no place to which to move. (Steinbeck, *Travels with Charley,* p. 26)

Many Americans do have some "place to which to move," but there are many in other countries who literally have no place to go when their land has no room for them. People displaced by large land holdings, usually the most productive lands, are left to fend for themselves. Many move to marginal lands in search of pastures and farmland. As population increases, even those marginal lands come under increased pressure.

In Kenya today, each farmer's land must be divided after his death among an average of four sons. In many areas, such subdivision has already reduced the average size of landholdings far below what can be efficiently farmed by one family. Much of the best land, moreover, is dedicated to growing cash crops for export, further intensifying the pressure on the land used for domestic food crops. (Ehrlich and Ehrlich, *Earth*, p. 84)

The loss of land drives many people to the cities, where in poor countries, population has increased much faster than jobs. The result is a large population living in shanties built from refuse and scouring the garbage dumps for food. Their hunger comes from having no other way to secure food.

The cause of hunger is not now, and will not be in the near future, a global shortage of food. Food is now available to all who can pay, and we know that there are huge surpluses rotting away. The problem is that so many cannot pay. The problem is also that those who have no money now have no access to land on which they could raise their own food. This land has been taken to raise crops or cattle for export, sometimes to the United States. (Daly and Cobb, *For the Common Good,* p. 279)

Many of the nations whose people are suffering from famine often are exporting food to pay off national debt. Others are purchasing military arms with food exports while their people are starving.

Meanwhile overgrazing and overcropping of land slowly turns the countryside into desert incapable of supporting life.

Dean Freudenberger wrote,

> Commitment to working for a world without hunger—a regenerative, just, and self-reliant agriculture for every nation—is needed because every agricultural economy that is based on export production is threatened by stress put on its land and resources. It is not practical to perpetuate a world agriculture that can no longer serve the needs of the earth and its people. . . . Peace will be achieved only when justice and integrity of the land coincide. (Freudenberger, *Global Dust Bowl,* p. 91)

A French experiment

An experiment in France gives an example of an attempt to bring together "justice and integrity of the land." France had the twin problems of farms that had become too small in the south and large-scale agri-business in the north. "A modest sum of capital was set aside to institute the Societe d'Amenagement Foncier d'Etablissement Rurale (SAFER), to staff it in agriculturally oriented provinces and empower it to purchase farmland that came into the open market. . . . In the southern provinces small, fragmented farms are purchased and traded so that they may be consolidated into larger and more productive units. In the north, larger acreages (hectares) are purchased and broken down into family-size units."

The new farms are appraised according to appropriate use, necessary improvements are made, and they are resold.

> Farm land purchase by speculators is prohibited. In addition, the owner must be the operator and must live continuously on the farm. There are no hobby farms. A new farm owner-operator is required to develop the enterprise within the defined limitations of topography and climate as established by SAFER during the process of consolidation and engineering. . . . Things have come

alive in rural France! Young people are going into farming. Rural communities offer quality living with amenities of every sort, and rural communities once again offer a good place to raise children. (Ibid., 95-97)

Creative Opportunities

If we worship God the Creator, we will care for the land *he* cares for. All around us are examples of hope that we can avoid a "Global Dust Bowl." There are plenty of opportunities to get creatively involved.

In Ghana, Tom Ahima runs his own "model" farm and "gives time to work for RURCON, an Africa-based network of Christian rural counselors. Traveling throughout Africa, he shares his years of farming experience with church development workers."

> Tom and his wife Agnes are outstanding farmers who have set up their own semi-mechanised model farm at Ofuman. . . . There they grow a variety of crops, including cassava (a root that is a staple of the national diet), maize, cashew nuts, aubergines and palm oil.
>
> Their vision is to use their 300 acre farm to help other farmers in the area, and nation, grow more and better crops. "It's part of the Christian spirit to be open and to share your ideas with others," he says. . . .
>
> One of Tom's particular concerns is to encourage educated young men to take up farming, which is seen by many to have a low social status. To this end, supported by a grant of £16,000 from Tear Fund, he has built a small hostel to accommodate graduate trainees who will spend a year learning first hand how to run a successful farm. (Rand, "A Harvest for Africa," *Tear Times*)

Development vs. relief

Art Beals is a relief and development specialist with World Concern. He has also worked in evangelism and church planting. He acknowledges that "relief" is necessary in the face of famine, but asks for "development" as well. The difference? *"Relief* would immediately establish a feeding program in the village. *Development,* on the other hand, would take time to observe, listen, and help the local populace to identify what meager resources they might have—resources which, if properly utilized and focused, might help them solve their own problem."

Listening comes first. If aid is dispensed paternalistically "from above," with no regard for people's innate knowledge or traditional methods, the fruits will be disappointing. Sally Farrant writes, "Africa is littered with broken down equipment and inappropriate schemes from the West. Traditional African methods are sensitive to climate and environment" (Farrant, "Enduring Hunger," *Tear Times).*

One development worker in the Philippines was sensitive and listened—and it paid off.

"It's either feast or famine," said one frustrated farmer.

The development worker asked him to explain.

"In the fruit-bearing season we have mangoes, pineapples, and oranges—far more than we can use for our own needs. But the markets are too far distant to sell our surplus to others."

It was true, there were no roads into the village, only seemingly endless mountain paths, narrow and steep.

"The fruit just rots on the ground in April and we are starving in November!"

The worker asked a few careful questions to help the community leaders discover their own solution.

"If we could save April's feast for November's famine," ventured one of the elders, "we would find life so much easier."

And that is just what they did. The solution to their dilemma was to be packaged in attractive jars labeled "Mountain Fresh Jams and Jellies." You can find them on the shelf of any major Manila supermarket and enjoy them on your breakfast toast in several of Manila's finest tourist hotels. (Beals, *Beyond Hunger,* pp. 90-91)

By listening carefully, the development worker was able to help the people become more self-sufficient, using the natural bounty of the land, without bringing in a form of technology incompatible with the natural environment.

A cooperative example

We don't all have the opportunity to help people in other cultures use their land more wisely. But we are all involved in some way in caring for land, whether our yards, company grounds, farms, or parks. And we can all ask ourselves if we are living in cooperation or competition with whatever "land" our lives touch.

In what spirit do we landscape our yards, plan the building or remodeling of our homes? How do we conduct ourselves in parks, in campgrounds, on trails? Do we have opportunities to be involved planning parks, playgrounds, even parking lots (does *every* tree have to go?) Where can we encourage planting or preserving trees in our communities? Do our churches look like they had to conquer nature in order to be built, or do they harmonize with their natural surroundings?

The original architect's plan for the Au Sable Institute of Environmental Studies showed a paved courtyard radiating from a central fountain with modern lighting fixtures illuminating everything. Hundreds of trees would have needed to be bulldozed down to bring the architect's "environmental" vision to reality.

The real Au Sable today is a group of rather rustic buildings in a stand of mature pine and aspen. When you are there you are *in* the woods. If you step back a little way from any building, it nearly disappears into the trees. "Sidewalks" are pine-chip paths delineated by small logs. The library/office building is built into a hillside and costs little to heat even in the bitter Michigan winters.

It would have been easier to mow down all the trees and start with a bare field; but the easier way is not what was chosen. The place was obviously built in a mood of cooperation *with* the land rather than triumph *over* it. As a result, the whole effect is one of quiet respect for the natural setting that God put there first.

Sabbath at Last

In 586 B.C., Jerusalem fell to King Nebuchadnezzar, who slaughtered many of the people, ransacked the temple, and took the remaining inhabitants into exile in Babylon to be his slaves. There the Jews stayed for seventy years while the land of their exile changed hands and came under the Persians.

After such a tragic story of suffering and destruction, the end of 2 Chronicles adds a curious note: "The land enjoyed its sabbath rests; all the time of its desolation it rested, until the seventy years were completed in fulfillment of the word of the LORD spoken by Jeremiah" (2 Chron. 36:21).

In the midst of the human tragedy, the Lord had not forgotten his long-ago commitment to the land: "In the seventh year the land is to have a sabbath of rest, a sabbath to the LORD" (Lev. 25:4). God still cared. One way or another, he saw to it that the land had rest.

And he still cares. Worshiping this God means caring for his land. It also means caring for his people, as we've begun to see in this chapter and will see more fully in the next. Land and people, both made by God, are inseparably connected.

CHAPTER ELEVEN
JUSTICE AND ECOLOGY

We hold these truths to be self-evident,
that all men are created equal;
that they are endowed by their Creator
with certain unalienable rights;
that among these, are life, liberty,
and the pursuit of happiness.
The Declaration of Independence

Who owns the moon?

That ethereal question has become very down-to-earth for Steve Goodman, a college student in Delaware who describes himself as "flat broke." He has a piece of the moon and he wants to sell it.

Twenty years ago, Goodman's father worked on space suits for the Apollo moon missions. After the Apollo 14 flight, Edward Goodman, Jr. supposedly ran a piece of tape down the pant leg of one suit, picking up "lint" that was really moon dust. He gave the 4-inch tape to his son, who now hopes to sell it for as much as $100,000.

"I figured if somebody was rich and wanted a conversation piece, that would be the thing for them," he says.

There's a catch. The National Aeronautics and Space Administration insists all 840 pounds of pebbles, soil, and stones brought back from the moon belongs to the U.S. government. *All* of it. It says so right on the books. "Clearly, according to our regulations, lunar dust is government property," says Gary Tesch, NASA's deputy legal counsel (Ashland, Wisconsin *Daily Press,* Jan. 6, 1992, p. 6).

Our astronauts found no "little green men" on the moon, a disappointment to decades of science-fiction buffs, though undoubtedly a relief to the astronauts. Our probes of Mars and Venus have turned up no signs of life either. But *what if* (as some speculate) there are microorganisms on Mars? When people finally land there, will we have the right to break off chunks of Mars and bring them back— even bring back some of the microorganisms? Will Mars be "ours"? Or does any form of indigenous life, no matter how humble, have exclusive claim to its own planet?

The Colonial Process

If thousands of years of human history offer any hint, we know exactly what will happen. Whoever lands on Mars first will take what they want and do what they want, so long as they have the power and means to do it. After all, any microorganisms (or any other life encountered there) will clearly be subhuman.

Bring that process back down to earth, and you have the essence of colonialism. Those with sufficient strength and money move into an area of land considered "uninhabited" and take what they want, considering the takings their own property because there are no other rightful claimants. There may be native people there, but if those natives have no concept of private land ownership, or if (even more convenient) they cannot put up a well-organized fight, then they are considered as having no valid claim to the land they live on.

When land is grabbed unjustly by those who only want what they can get out of it, it spells bad news for ecology.

"Two sides of the Christian coin"

The Moravian Church is the main indigenous evangelical church in Mosquitia in eastern Honduras, land of the deep rainforest. Most of Mosquitia's 40,000 Indians come from the Miskito tribe, and 80 percent of the Miskito Indians are Moravian Church members, the fruit of mission work in the 1930s. Their superintendent is Pastor Wilton Thomas, who oversees ten congregations.

Pastor Thomas has devoted ten years to translating the New Testament into the Miskito language. The Indians have lived for hundreds of years as hunter-gatherers in small isolated communities with close family ties. The rainforest and rivers give them game, fish, rice, beans, natural medicines, wood for fuel and for building homes and boats. But now Pastor Thomas is concerned that the Miskitos will soon be either dispersed or "working for landlords on land that once was theirs."

The reason? "Tens of thousands of hectares of land, traditionally used by Indian communities, have been cleared for large-scale cattle ranching or by peasant farmers to grow crops. As the forest is destroyed, so is the unique lifestyle of the Indians."

How is this happening?

Need and greed

Tear Fund (The Evangelical Alliance Relief Fund) is a Christian relief and development agency based in England. Its president is John Stott, well-known author, scholar, and rector emeritus of All Souls Church. The ministry of Tear Fund channels money and skilled personnel to indigenous churches and Christian organizations all over the world. There they help develop agriculture, well-drilling, cottage industries, health care, job training, and other efforts to help people help themselves.

Because we have supported its mission for twenty years and respect its integrity and low-key image, you'll find much information in this chapter coming from Tear Fund sources. From their close-up observations, Tear Fund workers identify five invaders of the Honduran rainforest "drawn by both greed and need":

- Cattle ranchers who clear the jungle to raise beef for American fast-food hamburgers;
- Logging companies who cut lucrative tropical hardwoods such as mahogany and teak;
- Business interests and prospectors for oil and gold;
- Peasant farmers (*campesinos*) who have left their farms in the south of Honduras as "ecological refugees" because their slash-and-burn farming methods have ruined the soil;
- International pressures of Honduras's enormous national debt (interest payments alone take up almost one quarter of the country's export earnings).

Clearly there is something deeper going on here than a few people deciding to cut a few trees because they need firewood.

"People here need their land to survive," says Pastor Thomas. "That is as important as the spiritual—there are two sides of the Christian coin" (Webb, "Death of the Rainforest," *Tear Times*).

There are long-term ecological effects of what is happening in places like Honduras—not only for the local area, but worldwide.

As the soil loses the binding influence of forest roots, it is soon washed away by the rains. When mountain slopes are cleared, the monsoon rush of water flows freely onto farmland, removing valuable topsoil, and leads to desertification.

The loss of moisture released into the air by large numbers of trees can change local patterns of rainfall. Some fear that this has contributed to drought conditions in areas of countries such as Haiti and Ethiopia.

Soil is washed into rivers, which become silted. During heavy rains these rivers may burst their banks and cause extensive flooding. Deforestation in Nepal is one cause of recent flooding in Bangladesh.

Every year, as much as two and a half billion tons of carbon dioxide are released from burning forests, adding to emissions from fossil fuels. As this gas traps the sun's heat in the atmosphere, scientists fear that the earth may grow warmer, melting polar ice and flooding low-lying coastal regions. ("Life and Death of the Rainforest," *Tear Times*)

A God of Justice

The promise was made in a magazine that came yesterday; it's there again, in an ad in today's mail. New Christian worship music promises to inspire such feelings of peace and joy (whether on hour-long cassette or CD) that it will bring the listener into the very presence of God.

Good feelings feel good. Sometimes, when circumstances happily come together, good feelings are a byproduct of worship. The Bible is realistic, and according to the Bible, the presence of God is a grittier place to be than that entered by plugging into your Walkman. The God of the Bible puts himself in the path of the injustices of earthly life and is involved in setting them right. This is the God who became man and stood up in the synagogue in his home town and announced:

"The Spirit of the Lord is on me,
 because he has anointed me
 to preach good news to the poor.
He has sent me to proclaim freedom for the prisoners
 and recovery of sight for the blind,

to release the oppressed,
    to proclaim the year of the Lord's favor." (Luke 4:18-19)

To be deeply involved with God means to be offended by injustice and to be involved in bringing about justice—somewhere, somehow, on some scale—because God is just.

One small solution: MOPAWI

Because of Christians' concern and action, something hopeful is happening in Mosquitia. MOPAWI (an abbreviation of the Miskito Indian words for "development of Mosquitia") is a new development agency based on Christian principles, and it is helping the Indians make a case for keeping their land, as well as preparing them to cope with the future as the world keeps moving in on them.

Andrew Leake, a Tear Fund environmentalist, has been instrumental in presenting the case for Indians' land rights before the Honduran government. Already some villages and forest land have been legally allocated to the Indians. "My hope and prayer is that we will succeed alongside the Indians in preserving their culture and allowing them to live as they want to," Leake says. "There have been some very depressing times. If I were not a Christian, I don't think I could carry on. I do believe very much that there is a strong Christian base for caring for the environment."

The development of the Mosquitia by outsiders is not going to stop; the Indians must learn to survive in the new environment. Therefore "MOPAWI . . . works with Indian communities on a range of long-term development projects to help them adapt to massive changes taking place" (Leake, "The Fight for Land Rights," *Tear Times*).

On the other side of the world, Christians are thinking of smaller-scale (but ingenious) ways to help the Honduran Indians. When the United Kingdom introduced a new five-pence coin in 1990, people complained that it was "too small and fiddly." Christian teenagers

invited people to give them the unpopular coins. They deposited
them at branches of the Midland Bank, which had set up a special
"Take Care" account. All the "Take Care" funds are going to help the
threatened Indian communities in the Honduran rainforest.

An odd word

"Eco-Justice" is an odd word. It looks and sounds like one of those
trendy terms invented to try to push two politically correct causes.
Actually it's what everything in this chapter has been about. It's a
word that makes sense, once we understand the connections it was
coined to express.

In 1990, the 202nd General Assembly of the Presbyterian Church
(U.S.A.) adopted a lengthy document on Christian responsibility
toward the creation. It begins with a helpful definition:

> The term "eco-justice"—ecology and justice—means ecological
> health and wholeness together with social and economic justice. It
> means the well-being of all humankind on a thriving earth. *(Res-
> toring Creation for Ecology and Justice,* p. 7)

"Eco-justice" is the recognition that "The heaven, even the
heavens, are the LORD's: but the earth hath he given to the children of
men" (Ps. 115:16, KJV). It means that the fate of human beings is tied
up with the fate of the earth, and what happens to one must affect the
other.

Injustice to people is often caused by poor ecological practices,
and bad ecology often results from injustice done to people; the two
are inseparably linked. "The Psalms and other books of the Bible
celebrate a radical relatedness. The Creator-Redeemer is so interre-
lated with the people and the nonhuman creation that together they
all rejoice—or mourn" *(Restoring Creation,* p. 5).

The prophet Isaiah looked ahead to the time of Judah's exile and
saw a vision of earth grown sick through human sin:

151

> The earth dries up and withers,
>> the whole world withers and grows sick,
>>> the earth's high places sicken,
>> and earth itself is desecrated by the feet of those who live in it,
> because they have broken the laws, disobeyed the statutes
>> and violated the eternal covenant.
> For this a curse has devoured the earth;
>> and its inhabitants stand aghast. . . .
> The earth reels to and fro like a drunken man
>> and sways like a watchman's shelter;
>> the sins of men weigh heavy upon it,
>>> and it falls to rise no more. (Isa. 24:4-6a, 20, NEB)

Isaiah's words have come true in places beyond Judah. In many places the land is "desecrated" because "the sins of men weigh heavy upon it."

Cocoa Beans and Bananas

When we were married, I (Sandy) had no idea that the sugar on the store shelves was anything but "the pure cane sugar from Hawaii" they sang about in the commercials. It was a surprise to hear Dale talk about his parents laboring alongside Mexican migrant workers in the depression, harvesting sugar *beets*—in *Minnesota,* yet.

We often host a weekly Bible study in our home, and last year we led a study on a Christian view of ecology (from our NetWork studyguide *Tending Creation*). At these studies there's always a hot-water pot at the ready with coffee, tea, sugar, and cocoa—which turns out to be ironic if not downright inconsistent. The sugar probably comes from next door in Minnesota, but the other products come from tropical regions. Those old schoolbook maps that showed the symbol of a coffee bean over Colombia, or a tea leaf over Ceylon, were true-to-life.

Since grade school geography classes where we were taught to identify a country with a single crop—bananas with El Salvador, coffee with Brazil, cocoa with Ghana—most of us have come to see an underdeveloped country's concentration on one or two export crops as practically God-ordained. In reality, there is nothing "natural" about the concentration on a few, largely low-nutrition crops. (Lappe and Collins, *World Hunger: Ten Myths,* p. 21)

During the era of colonization, the lands of South America, the Caribbean, and Africa were claimed by European countries that considered them undeveloped and unoccupied; the few natives who were found there were not considered as having any rights to the land. Governments granted large areas to certain people and companies to develop the land in order to meet market needs in the home country. Thus colonial land worldwide came to be "owned" by European landowners.

A few concentrated crops were picked by colonial powers to be grown in the colonies solely because they would pay. They were high-profit crops for the high-paying markets—not local markets but markets back home. The policy was good for money-making but bad for the land and the people who lived on it.

In the last century, Europe divided Africa and set aside the best land to grow the crops Europe wanted. For example Kenya was planted with coffee plantations and Sudan with cotton. Local farmers were pushed onto poorer land.

When independence came these "cash crops" were maintained to earn foreign exchange so that oil and machinery needed for development could be bought. Then in the world recession during the 1970's, these countries were forced to borrow. Demand for their crops, which Europe had planted, fell, while prices of essential imports like oil increased. Many countries were unable to repay their loans and today still carry large international debts.

Meanwhile, the best farm land is often given over to these crops and local people try to survive on "marginal" lands. (Farrant, "Enduring Hunger," *Tear Times*)

The problem is not shortage of land, but inappropriate use of land. It could grow food for local people but instead is given over to money-making export crops. "The same land now made to grow cocoa, coffee, rubber, tea, or sugar could grow an incredible diversity of nutritious crops—grains, high-protein legumes, vegetables, fruits and root crops" (Lappe and Collins, *World Hunger,* p. 21).

The new colonialism
Intensive single-crop agriculture for home markets was practiced in the colonies until the 1960s, when political revolutions threw off colonialism and brought independence to many Third World countries.

The land, however, did not automatically revert to small farmers growing their own food after the revolutions. A new kind of "colonialization" moved in to continue to drain the land.

The international business organizations were quick to fill the vacuum created by decolonization. As the Western European colonial ministries withdrew to Europe, international business firms—accountable to no one—moved in. Western industries needed raw materials. So even though the Western nations relinquished political control, the business firms exerted economic control. Neocolonialism was born. Agriculture and other production is still run for the benefit of global markets, generating wealth for corporations and their stockholders. Outsiders continue to control indigenous peoples and occupy their land. . . . The situation is now compounded by the new realities of international debt, debt service, and trade deficits. Colonialism and neocolonialism continue to bear the fruits of poverty, injustice, and desertification. (Freudenberger, *Global Dust Bowl,* p. 81)

On the surface it appears that money provided for agricultural development ought to *improve* a country's ability to feed itself. In reality it often doesn't work that way.

> We have come . . . to the painful conclusion that very little of First World development effort in the Third World, and even less of business investment, has been actually beneficial to the majority of the Third World's people. On the whole, just as government policy in the United States has driven most farmers off the land while enriching a few, so development policies in the Third World have made many landless, filled the vast slums surrounding Third World cities, and added to the problem of hunger. (Daly and Cobb, *For the Common Good,* pp. 289-290)

People who are driven from their homelands to make way for outside development go in search of water and food for their livestock and land to carry on their subsistence farming.

In the dryer lands of Africa's Sahel, the southern fringe of the Sahara Desert, the search for water is absolutely vital. When water is scarce, the surrounding vegetation can't spring back from being trampled and overgrazed. The few trees animals don't eat are consumed by the cooking fire. War in the area compounds the agony; herdsmen can no longer travel freely in search of water. All this time the desert encroaches, leaving even fewer resources for the herdsmen and their cattle (see Ehrlich and Ehrlich, *Earth,* pp. 79-82).

At the other end of Africa, a former Peace Corps worker returning to Malawi noticed the "empty hills, plowed valleys and plains" and the absence of trees. "What happened to the trees?" he asks. "They were cut down for two reasons: for fuel and to make room for more planting of corn (cornmeal flour is a staple ingredient in Malawi diet). The effect is dramatic—it seems as though the entire southern region of the country, where more than half the people live, has been deforested."

Land is continually stripped of its forests and subjected to overuse by people with no other means of survival. One farmer, pointing to a hillside of trees, said, "If the Forestry Department hadn't stopped them, the people would have taken those too." The people have no other way to cook (Theroux, "Malawi: Faces of A Quiet Land," *National Geographic*).

No hope in the cities

With no productive land to farm or graze, and nowhere else to go, rural peasants turn to the cities in hope of finding work. Unfortunately, unemployment is already rampant in the city. The move becomes only another disappointment. In many cases "the newly arrived rural family moves into the already crowded slum dwelling of relatives or friends. A paper and tin shack. A single water tap on a distant street corner. Open sewers. Fetid heaps of decaying debris. Noise. Pollution. Crime. Prostitution. This is what the hope-filled farmer receives in exchange for his rural poverty" (Beals, *Beyond Hunger*, p. 56).

A Toxic Circle

You may be thinking, *All this talk about injustice in other countries has very little to do with me. I didn't establish colonialism. I don't own these huge plantations. I'm not responsible for what's happening halfway around the world.*

You may not be responsible, but you are affected.

Thirty years ago in *Silent Spring*, Rachel Carson sounded an early warning about the dangers of pesticides. She wrote of towns where robins and other birds were found dead on the lawns, where squirrels and even cats were found dead. She warned that the threat extended even to humans through pesticides in our food.

Since *Silent Spring* much progress has been made in banning and getting rid of pesticides. But the problem is back, through the back door. Even though our government stopped mass aerial spraying and banned the use of the most dangerous pesticides in the United States, chemical companies are still manufacturing them and shipping them overseas.

[The Environmental Protection Agency] prohibits pesticide sales in the United States if a chemical is suspected of causing cancer or birth defects in humans, if it harms fish and wildlife or accumulates in soil and water. But the Federal Insecticide, Fungicide and Rodenticide Act *permits chemical manufacturers to export pesticides* that are banned, restricted or refused registration at home because of extreme toxicity. Up to 150 million pounds of these blacklisted products worth more than $800 million—about one fourth of U.S. pesticide production—are marketed overseas each year. (emphasis added)

Is this just? Toxic products, too dangerous for us but apparently O.K. for the rest of the world, are "sold to many nations including Thailand, Chile, Indonesia, France, Italy, Great Britain, Japan and New Zealand" to be "used on various crops including rice, apples, pears, pineapples, wine grapes, beer hops and tea that in turn are exported to the United States."

Our injustice returns to us; there's a "toxic twist." Banned from the U.S., exported overseas, the poisons "return to the United States on imported meats and produce, completing what environmentalists have dubbed the 'circle of poison'" (Satchell, "A Vicious 'Circle of Poison,'" *U.S. News & World Report*).

The U.S. could ban the manufacture of the pesticides here, but that would only move their manufacture to another country. As long as maximum profit is the goal, some way will be found to circumvent any obstacle to production and sales. Profit becomes the filter through which acts are evaluated. Morality and justice become irrelevant.

How different it would be if justice were the standard by which pesticide manufacture were judged.

The point is not to condemn manufacturing or profit-making or the chemical industry as inherently evil. The point is that practices such as the "circle of poison" cannot be reconciled with "tilling and keeping" the earth. They are not "serving" the land or the people, and they are not "guarding" anything except the profit of a few.

House to house and field to field

The drive for the "profit of a few" leads to accumulating land and draining its resources, which leads in turn to injustice for the people who once farmed the land for their own sustenance. The prophet Isaiah spoke out against remarkably similar injustice in his own time. "Woe to you who add house to house and join field to field till no space is left and you live alone in the land" (Isa. 5:8). How would Isaiah respond if he knew, for example, that 93 percent of arable lands in Latin America are held by a mere 7 percent of land owners? (Goldsmith and Hildyard, *The Earth Report,* p. 130).

Isaiah saw that abuse of land will naturally accompany land-grabbing: "A ten-acre vineyard will produce only a bath of wine, a homer of seed only an ephah of grain" (Isa. 5:10). That works out to about six gallons of wine to an acre of vineyard and three-fifths of a bushel of grain from six bushels of seed. Abused land does not last as long as productive land.

It is sometimes argued that if economic growth is limited, poor people will be condemned to continued poverty or even starvation. Bill McKibben provides an interesting response to that argument:

> I am dubious about the actual depth of feeling for the Third World implied by such arguments—they mesh too conveniently with our desires. After all, limiting our standard of living and sharing our wealth would also help alleviate poverty, and an overheated, ozone-depleted world will probably be even crueler to the poor than to the rich. A humble path, in which rich world meets the poor world halfway, seems to me to allow for far more justice than an ever-growing supply of air conditioners. *We don't need to choose between cruelty and the greenhouse effect; there are more rational, if more difficult, ways to show our love of our fellow man.* (McKibben, *The End of Nature,* p. 203, emphasis added)

Their Own Fault?

There's another logical question to ask: Don't poor farmers get themselves into their hopeless situations by deliberately letting large corporations in? A subsistence farmer is barely making it, and along comes a sugar exporter or coffee exporter who offers a good price for his land or good wages if he starts growing only sugar or coffee. If he sells out, isn't the resulting situation his own fault?

But Isaiah did not ask *how* the huge landholders got their land. Even if the land is taken in a way that is technically legal, there is still the matter of greed. Isaiah said "woe" to those who grasp for all they can get and don't give others a chance.

Jeremiah, a contemporary of Isaiah, gave a similar warning when Judah had fallen into sin: "This is what the Lord says: 'The whole land will be ruined, though I will not destroy it completely. Therefore the earth will mourn and the heavens above grow dark'" (Jer. 4:27-28a). Joel, Amos, and Micah all added their voices, warning that the sin and injustice of Israel would bring destruction on the land and poverty to the people.

A "liberal" bent?

If ownership of all the land by the few is unjust, do we achieve justice by distributing all the land equally? At this point the argument begins to sound suspiciously Marxist. "Land reform" sounds like a leftist Communist demand, something Christians should shy away from.

Art Beals of World Concern has heard the objection before:

American evangelicals all too often seem amazingly uncomfortable with the very word . . . *justice.*

Mention it and you sometimes are thought of as a leftist, a theological liberal, or a revolutionary! Perhaps this results from our obsession with material wealth, our uninformed or unrealistic views concerning the broad reach of human poverty, and the possibility that our affluent, consumptive life styles may have some relationship to the poverty of others.

Can a small minority of earth's people control and use a vast majority of the resources and consider itself just? (Beals, *Beyond Hunger,* pp. 118-119)

We've already read about how God provided for a "jubilee" every fifty years, when land reverted to its original owner family. In that way and many other ways the law provided for people to live together justly.

True Spirituality

We need to be cautious of a gospel that only deals with personal righteousness. Such a "gospel" can too easily fit comfortably into a lifestyle of self-absorption that excuses rather than confronts injustice. If we really serve God as we claim, we will care for other people who live on the land God has entrusted to all of us.

In Isaiah's time the Israelites sought a more "spiritual" life. The problem was, they were seeking the "spiritual" life as something separate from real life, an experience that had little to do with their personal relationships with either each other or God. They were like New Agers who get together and "visualize" an end to world hunger but do nothing tangible to help hungry people—and even go on consuming as much as before. Evangelicals can be equally guilty of complacency when we gather at prayer retreats seeking only a deeper devotional life—or comfortably curl up with tapes that bring us into "the presence of God."

For day after day they seek me out;
    they seem eager to know my ways,
as if they were a nation that does what is right
    and has not forsaken the commands of its God.

They ask me for just decisions
   and seem eager for God to come near them.
"Why have we fasted," they say,
   "and you have not seen it?
Why have we humbled ourselves,
   and you have not noticed?" (Isa. 58:2-3)

God had a different version of the truly spiritual life. His vision of genuine spirituality was—and still is— one of people treating people justly because they see in each other the image of God.

Is not this the kind of fasting I have chosen:
to loose the chains of injustice
   and untie the cords of the yoke,
to set the oppressed free
   and break every yoke?
Is it not to share your food with the hungry
   and to provide the poor wanderer with shelter? (Isa. 58:6-7)

The prophet Micah said the same more succinctly: "He has showed you, O man, what is good. And what does the LORD require of you? To act justly and to love mercy and to walk humbly with your God" (Mic. 6:8).

We know that God cares about justice because his law provides for the protection of poor people from those who would take advantage of them. For example, wages were to be paid by sunset (Deut. 24:15). When a loan was made, a common practice was to put up a garment as security, but each day the lender was to carry out an act of kindness and respect to the debtor: the garment was to be returned at night, "because his cloak is the only covering he has for his body. What else will he sleep in?" (Exod. 22:26-27; see also Deut. 24:12-13).

The law of gleaning diffused landowners' possible greed by providing for the sharing of the harvest:

When you are harvesting in your field and you overlook a sheaf, do not go back to get it. Leave it for the alien, the fatherless and the widow, so that the LORD your God may bless you in all the work of your hands. When you beat the olives from your trees, do not go over the branches a second time. Leave what remains for the alien, the fatherless and the widow. When you harvest the grapes in your vineyard, do not go over the vines again. Leave what remains for the alien, the fatherless and the widow. (Deut. 24:19-21)

The practice of gleaning was good for both the landowners and the gleaners. The gleaners received the produce in a way that encouraged their responsibility and preserved their dignity: they had to go out and work for it. The landowner became a giver and also got a clean field or vineyard.

Many farmers in Third World countries—and many Third World governments—are enslaved by debt. For that matter, our own farmers and our own government aren't in such great shape either, debt-wise.

In God's law, among the Israelites, no one could be ruined forever by debt, and no one could grow permanently rich on someone else's debt. There was a provision for the regular canceling of debts. "At the end of every seven years you must cancel debts. This is how it is to be done: Every creditor shall cancel the loan he has made to his fellow Israelite. He shall not require payment from his fellow Israelite or brother, because the LORD's time of canceling debts has been proclaimed" (Deut. 15:1-2).

For those of us with fifteen-year mortgages on our homes, the cancellation of debts every seven years sounds pretty good. Aren't we talking about a radical reformation of financial practices? Is that practical?

We don't have a proposal for a new world financial system. But there are many practical ideas for living every day in ways that help rather than hurt the economy of our planetary "house."

CHAPTER TWELVE
HOW SIMPLE DOES SIMPLE HAVE TO BE?

It's okay to be a little poor.
It's a little more sane.
Ken Raspotnik,
Wisconsin sheep farmer

For years our water-meter reader visited us once a month because he had to come into the house to read the meter. The meter was an artistic brass creation in the bathroom, and in order to read the dial he had to bend down with his head next to the toilet. He never complained. But once on the way out he remarked, "Your water meter's like the rest of your house. Antique and obsolete."

The water company has installed a new meter. It's still in the bathroom, but now it has wires running outside the house to a little black box that is "read" with an electronic gun. The rest of our house, as far as we know, is still antique and obsolete.

Twenty Miles Out

It seems some people just can't shake their image.

A new family in church was invited to our home for Sunday dinner. Before they came over, they warned their two sons: "Now don't expect to watch TV this afternoon because the Larsens don't have one."

"How do you know?" the boys asked.

"We can just tell," was the reply. In fact they were right, but how did they *know*?

People who meet us always think we live in an old farmhouse twenty miles out and heat with wood and grow our own food, none of which is true, except that most summers we do have a small garden. People think this even if we are dressed up in our best clothes and attempting to look sophisticated.

The truth is, we know too much to be enamored with that sort of life. We know too many people who are living (or have tried) the "simple" life and found it's a lot more complicated than it's cracked up to be. If you live twenty miles out nobody from town will ever come to see you, and you spend immense amounts of time in your car, and nothing is dirtier or takes more time and is more work than heating with wood, and growing your own food is an all-consuming task.

"Adopting a simple lifestyle,"—"living more simply"—is often prescribed as the only way to save the earth. There are books telling Christians how to achieve it. But what does it mean to live simply? And is it the answer?

Simple or not?

I (Sandy) first heard the term "simple lifestyle" fifteen years ago from the mouth of our pastor at the time, and heard it—surprising-ly—applied to *ourselves*.

The house we were renting very reasonably was going to be sold; we had to move. We looked at apartments around town in Evanston, Illinois, but none of the apartment buildings would rent to us because their monthly rent was more than 25 percent of our monthly income.

One morning I came in to the church office where I worked and reported to the pastor that we still hadn't found a place, and why. The pastor kindly phoned the manager of the apartment building we liked best to put in a good word for us.

Then I heard him say, "This couple leads a very simple lifestyle."

I had never heard the phrase before, but when I figured out what it meant, I was stunned. We had recently returned to the U.S. from two years in Europe, living what we thought of as very sparingly. *Now* we had a car, a phone, a huge apartment with a full-sized refrigerator, a closetful of clothes—things we could never have afforded before. We had to drive or ride our bikes everywhere because public transportation wasn't convenient. We had jobs we had to report to every day. Simple? We thought life had gotten very cumbersome.

More than fifteen years later, our "lifestyle" would be called "simple" compared with most of the people around us. We live in a house with no central heating, basement, garage, TV, VCR, cable, microwave, portable phone, or power lawn mower. On the other hand, it's a house where people walk in the door and say "Wow!" at the jewel-red velvets, the restored Victrola, the Victorian furniture, the amazing lamps.

Look around at the overstuffed chair found in the alley, refinished and reupholstered in tapestry; the unique clothes from Ragstock, a one-of-a-kind used-clothing shop in Duluth; the Oriental wool carpet from the Holy Family Church flea market. Are we living simply, or aren't we? That's a good question.

This "simplicity" may only reflect a need to surround ourselves with well-used, human-touched things. It may reflect self-satisfaction in making usable what somebody else deemed useless. Most likely it's a practical way of coping with expensive taste on a low income.

"Cash within 90 days"

When we began writing for pay, the checks from our first publisher bore the inscription, "Please Cash within 90 Days." Ha! Ha! Ninety minutes was more like it. They say that in writing you can make a killing, but you can't make a living, which is why we live up here at the end of the world where housing is cheap and the pressures to consume are lower than in more populous parts of the country. (It would be interesting to see, if this book became a best seller and made us a nice amount of money, whether and how much our life-style would change.)

"Simple" depends on perspective. Why are we so rich when there are committed Christians in other parts of the world who have to walk miles to the well, cannot afford books or clothes for school, have no transportation but their feet?

Which is all to say, even if we all agree we should live simply, no one can legislate for anyone else what level "simplicity" means. One of our neighbors might think our life is weighed down with unnecessary items; another might wonder how we get by on so little. And they would probably both be right.

Pastimes of the rich and famous

Any attempt to define "simple lifestyle" is full of paradox. The irony of living in this area of uncertain work is that the less employed you are, the more freedom you have to enjoy the playful pastimes of the rich. Nearly everybody has a boat of some kind, and Lake Superior is at our front door; miles of deep forest surround us; stunning vistas are everywhere. People in high tax brackets work all year so they can come here for two weeks to play. If you are willing to accept a lower-income life, you can play here year round. People wait all year to come here for a week's skiing vacation; in winter we can ski for free nearly every day. On the National Forest trails we use there's no instructor to give you lessons or ski patrol to rescue you, no hot tub waiting at the end of the loop. But neither are there crowds, short-tempered staff, or noisy partiers in the next room. The only noise is the roar of snowmobiles on the trails that intersect the ski trails (and *that's* a clash of cultures that will never be settled).

"Give me neither poverty nor riches," prayed Agur son of Jakeh in Proverbs, "but give me only my daily bread. Otherwise, I may have too much and disown you and say, 'Who is the LORD?' Or I may become poor and steal, and so dishonor the name of my God" (Prov. 30:8-9). Likewise Jesus instructed us to pray, "Give us today our daily bread" (Matt. 6:11). It is a reasonable prayer. We are not to deny or ignore our needs; we are to acknowledge them and ask God to meet them. But we are not to demand that God go further than that.

How Much Is Enough?

We're to live in balance between neediness and extravagance. Then what's the "right" level? Somewhere between Donald Trump and Mother Theresa, but we must get more specific than that. *How much* should we earn? *How much* should we own?

"How much?" is a *quantitative* question. It demands a legalistic solution: give me a figure, a statistic, a load limit. Don't bother me about philosophy; just tell me, how far can I go?

"Feed me with the food that is needful for me," the RSV translates Proverbs 30:8. It seems reasonable to answer "how much?" with "just what I need."

But what do you *need?* Food enough to maintain health, clothing to keep you decent, shelter to keep you dry and warm. (Or cool, if you live in the South; looking at three feet of snow outside, it's hard to remember there are places where people *want* to be cool.)

What else do people *need?* Transportation (but only to places you *need* to go). What kind of transportation? Bus? Bicycle? Car? What *kind* of car?—that question could consume a whole book in itself!

Speaking of books, do you *need* books? How many? What quality? Do you have to *own* books, or should you only use the library? If you don't buy books, what will happen to *our* income? How will *we* as authors buy the things we need?

Most of us do not need most of the things we own in the sense of needing them for physical survival. But there are needs beyond bare survival. We have aesthetic needs, emotional needs. We need art and beauty around us; we need tangible reminders of people and events; we need intellectual stimulation; we need play; we need conveniences so that our lives are free of endless drudgery.

167

But then most of us have those things to some degree.

Yet when asked, "How much do you need?" most of us would answer, "Just a little bit more."

In D.H. Lawrence's story "The Rocking-Horse Winner," a young English family never has quite enough money to keep up the social position the mother desires. Their house is haunted by a silent whisper from every corner: "There *must* be more money! There *must* be more money!" The young son, Paul, mysteriously finds his way to "luck" and secretly makes money betting on horse races. He arranges to give his mother thousands of pounds anonymously, and she spends it on every luxury she has ever wanted. But something surprising happens. The whispers in the house grow shrill and mad, "like a chorus of frogs on a spring evening." "There *must* be more money!" they scream. "There *must* be more money!—more than ever! More than ever!" (Lawrence, "The Rocking-Horse Winner," *The Oxford Book of Short Stories*).

Does *anybody* have "enough?" More accurately, does anybody *feel* he or she has "enough"?

This Christmas we had trouble thinking of anything we wanted for Christmas presents. Until, of course, we started looking in store windows or noticing what other people own. Though our income is less than many of the people around us, we find that we are perfectly satisfied with what we have—*as long as* we keep our eyes off the possessions of other people. Or, more accurately, as long as we keep our eyes off the status and peer relationships that the possessions of other people purchase for them.

When our estimate of ourselves is tied to the possession of certain goods, we live in insecurity. We could lose them at any time. Or other people could up the ante by getting what we don't have. Or what's "in" could become "out."

In Sinclair Lewis's novel, George F. Babbitt finds his righteousness in possessing the right things—that is, things identical to those possessed by his neighbors in Floral Heights, Ohio, in 1920. Soaking himself in his tiled bathroom, Babbitt is lulled by luxury.

The drain-pipe was dripping, a dulcet and lively song: drippety drip drip dribble, drippety drip drip drip. He was enchanted by it. He looked at the solid tub, the beautiful nickel taps, the tiled walls of the room, and felt virtuous in the possession of this splendor. (Sinclair Lewis, *Babbitt,* p. 80)

Babbitt will go through a religious phase before the book is over, but his response in the bathtub is not a biblical response. To have a genuinely Christian answer, the question, "How much?" has to be answered *qualitatively,* not *quantitatively.* What kind of life best displays the virtues of Christ? What kind of life is most consistent with the values God desires to develop in our character?

When those questions are answered, and only after those questions are answered, can we approach the question "How much?" from a quantitative side and start talking about dollars, square feet, and how many holes for cars there should be in the garage.

Enforced Simplicity

Attempts to legislate simplicity have tended to go sour. The American Puritans shunned ostentation, but their ideals of humility and moderation ran into conflict with their own increasing wealth. In 1634 the General Court of Massachusetts Bay attempted to enforce simplicity of dress:

The Court, taking into consideration the great, superfluous, & unnecessary expenses occasioned by reason of some new & immodest fashions, as also the wearing of silver, gold, & silk laces, girdles, hatbands, etc., hath therefore ordered that no person, either man or woman, shall hereafter make or buy any apparel, either woolen, or silk, or linen, with any lace on it, silver, gold, silk, or thread, under the penalty of forfeiture of such clothes. (quoted in David E. Shi, *In Search of the Simple Life,* p. 26)

169

By 1651 the Court members had to admit that their declaration "hath not yet taken that effect which were to be desired." On the contrary, "We cannot but to our grief take notice that intolerable excess & bravery hath crept in upon us, & *especially amongst people of mean condition*" (emphasis added). Ostentation was now particularly offensive among people of lower rank. The Court members saw their duty "to declare our utter detestation & dislike that *men & women of mean condition, educations & callings* should take upon the garb of gentlemen, by the wearing of gold or silver lace, or buttons, or points at their knees, to walk in great boots; or women of the same rank to wear silk or tiffany hoods or scarves, *which though allowable to persons of greater estates, or more liberal education yet we cannot but judge it intolerable to persons of such like condition*"(emphasis added). The declaration went on to set precise limits no one whose financial estate was under 200 pounds could wear such items as gold, silver, and silk (ibid. 26-27).

We shouldn't be too hard on the Puritans, whose stereotype of rigid legalism is not entirely fair. They endured persecution for their belief in the authority of Scripture and salvation by faith. Their journals show they struggled immensely with whether or not they were of the elect. In their communities they strove to demonstrate the holiness of God's covenant people.

In fact the Puritan "dress codes" resemble the *unwritten* law against ostentation observed in most churches.

Blue hair in church?

For a while a few years ago, women were getting their hair dyed—not just to cover gray, but dyed unnatural colors. Like pink or green.

A hairdresser of our acquaintance showed up with blue hair and second thoughts. "It looked really nice in my shop," she moaned. "But I can't go to church till it grows out. What would people say?"

She was probably right. People would probably have said it was ostentatious . . . or worldly . . . or weird . . . or in bad taste . . . or something. But she should have gone to church anyway. I (Sandy) once showed up at Sunday-night choir practice with pink hair because I had been in a Sunday-afternoon performance of "Godspell," and nobody said anything (at least not to me). But then, everybody knows theater people are weird.

Most churches have an unspoken understanding of just *how* showy the members are allowed to be in the way they dress, the cars they drive, the jewelry they wear, the things they own. If you look closely, somewhere in that code (like the Puritan code) there really are categories for *who* can wear or own *how much*. So-and-So can get away with it; So-and-So Else can't. We confess we are particularly disturbed (and jealous?) when we see people we *know* can't afford it driving new cars or otherwise living beyond their means.

At least the Puritans wrote their rules down.

Simplicity Attempted

In our ministry in southern California in the late 1960s, then in Europe in the early 1970s, we met many hippie attempts at simplified communal living, sometimes with Christian intentions.

The hippies were mystified at why everybody in straight society thought it was necessary to work so hard. After all, if milk cost (at that time) a dollar a gallon, and bread was fifty cents, and you could rent an old house for a hundred dollars a month, and ten or twelve people could live there, why would any of them have to work more than an hour or so a day to take care of all their needs?

Few hippies were students of history. They could have learned something from other American attempts at communal simplicity. These attempts were always idealistic and nearly always fell apart.

In New England in the first part of the nineteenth century, the Transcendental movement strove to elevate the self above crass material pursuits. Ralph Waldo Emerson and Henry David Thoreau chose to pursue their simple lives in solitude (though both socialized

171

more widely and often than is usually imagined). Some Transcendentalists envisioned communities where many hands would divide the work, making leisure time for contemplation and artistic creation.

One of the more Spartan attempts at communal simple living was the "Fruitlands" farm, ninety acres near the village of Harvard, Massachusetts. In the summer of 1843, Bronson Alcott, the English journalist Charles Lane, their families, and a few other hardy experimenters went to Fruitlands to begin their ideal Transcendental community. The plan was to combine plain living with high thinking. Their days together were to be spent working, studying, and engaging in philosophical conversation.

We have an insider's look at life at Fruitlands, because one of the four daughters of Bronson Alcott was the writer Louisa May Alcott. Her record of life on the farm is far from romanticized:

> Such farming probably was never seen before since Adam delved. The band of brothers began by spading garden and field; but a few days of it lessened their ardor amazingly. Blistered hands and aching backs suggested the expediency of permitting the use of cattle 'til the workers were better fitted for noble toil by a summer of the new life. . . . The sowing was equally peculiar, for, owing to some mistake, the three brethren, who devoted themselves to this graceful task, found when about half through the job that each had been sowing a different sort of grain in the same field; . . . after a long consultation and a good deal of laughter, it was decided to say nothing and see what would come of it.

Another Fruitlands resident "held that all the emotions of the soul should be freely expressed" and set about freely expressing them; still another preferred to go naked, but was repressed by the other members of the community and by sunburn (from Shi, *In Search of the Simple Life*, pp. 162-163).

Simple communal living, as an end in itself, appears doomed to disillusionment and failure.

Life with the Bedouins

Near Riyadh, Saudi Arabia, an American couple named Wayne and Patti Eastep lived for six weeks with a Bedouin clan, the Al Amrah, known as the "nomads of the nomads." The Easteps crammed Arabic and learned all they could about the Bedouin, for there were two conditions on their living with the clan: they would have no interpreter, and they would live as Bedouins.

The Al Amrah clan consists of the families of ten brothers. The camp with which the Easteps traveled included about 150 people living in a dozen tents. From fall to early summer the Al Amrah migrate with their camels, goats, and sheep over a 750-mile-long area of desert, searching for grass and water, moving every few days, usually going about fifteen miles per day. They use trucks for transportation and carrying water, but their self-sufficient economy depends on their flocks and herds.

The Easteps' thermometer burst at 125 degrees; at night the temperature "cooled" to 90. They were constantly thirsty, and flies swarmed everywhere; but for a childless American couple married fifteen years, it was most difficult to adjust to the lack of privacy. They were "seldom alone except when performing bodily functions" since the Bedouins live, eat, and travel communally.

Their attitude toward possessions is shaped by the desert. Whatever is necessary for survival is treated with utmost care, even reverence—such things as rugs to sit on, bolsters to lean on, an incense burner to perfume hair and clothing, a large pot of hot water for making endless cups of tea and coffee and for cleaning dishes, brightly painted platters for *kipsa* [a communal rice-and-lamb dish], omnipresent bowls of dates. Toward everything else, including money, they are relatively indifferent. . . . With the Bedouin, money is communal; all share according to need. (Eastep, "Nomads of the Desert," *Smithsonian)*

The Bedouins' priorities gradually rubbed off on their American guests. When the Easteps arrived, they could barely fit all their camping gear and clothing into their jeep. By the time they left to drive 900 miles north to live briefly with another clan, "we were pulling over to the side of the road at night, taking out our grass mat and sleeping bags and settling down in the sand" (ibid.).

Americans would call Bedouin life "simple," despite their ornate coffeepots and rugs. Why has their communal life worked for thousands of years when places like Fruitlands and most hippie communes survived only a few years?

A Solid Base

The Bedouin clan is based not on some idealistic view of human nature or a desire to shed material goods, but rather on *committed relationships* among an extended family where everyone knows where he or she belongs in the hierarchy. All are mutually interdependent and know it.

In the hippie communes the commitment was to self, or to freedom. Accepting a role or a goal defined by someone else would have been unthinkable.

The Amish live simply in their self-contained communities, and their way of life endures because they are *committed to God and to one another.* The evidence is that in order to sustain itself, the simple life must be lived as a *result* of a commitment to a higher goal—rather than as the goal itself.

In Chapter 9 we made the point that as Christians we are committed to a life of worship and trust in God. Our worship and trust should naturally bring us into community with like-minded people, and we should become committed to them also.

174

Along the way, those commitments are very likely to produce a simplified way of living. True simplicity will come when we are satisfied that *we already have enough* in Christ and in one another. Simplicity is the knowledge of sufficiency rather than the nagging consciousness of insufficiency.

Christians do not necessarily have to live together "in tents" like the Bedouin. But we should have similar "intents" of commitment to taking care of one another and the mutual sharing of resources.

Simplicity—a by-product of satisfaction

If simplicity is pursued as an aim in itself, it winds up just as materialistic as the life it claims to avoid. Why? Because the focus remains on *the material:* beans instead of roast, paper instead of plastic, thrift shop instead of boutique, old Fiesta instead of new Acura. We end up either with a martyr complex ("poor me") or self-righteous ("what a terrific me"). In either case the emphasis is on the *things* being denied or given up.

When simple living happens as a *result* of having a higher aim, a cause bigger than oneself, then it is done with joy—the by-product of the fulfillment of giving ourselves to a higher cause. Simplicity happens naturally when we are satisfied with something else, something more important than material gain.

While this book was being written, Mother Theresa fell ill with heart problems and pneumonia. She is the example of "simplicity" who immediately comes to most people's minds. She and her sisters live simply—but not because they have set out to make a point about a "simple lifestyle." They live that way because they desire to live like the people to whom they are ministering in Jesus' name. She says, "We serve Him when we care for Him among the poor; we love Him best when we love those who need Him most" (Beals, *Beyond Hunger,* p. 179).

It makes all the difference in the world whether we choose work for the purpose we find in it instead of the money we make by it. When we are doing the work we love to do for the God we believe in, we have neither time nor interest for rampant consumption.

Simplicity and self-interest

Fine, but let's focus on ecology again. Time is short and resources are limited. Shouldn't we all be living simply as a practical matter of survival, *in order to save the earth?*

In *The Simple Life: A Christian Stance Toward Possessions,* Church of the Brethren clergyman Vernard Eller questions: 1. whether that works; and 2. whether that motive is sufficient for Christians.

There is a parallel, Eller says, with smoking. People have been warned for decades that smoking is dangerous. Logically, they know they should quit. The dangers of smoking are even more certain and immediate than the threat of our general environmental problems; the cure is far simpler than curing our environmental problems. Yet most smokers won't give up smoking—*not even for their own survival.* "If commanding self-interest can't lead us even to give up a noisome weed, what possible chance is there that, before we are forced to do so, it will lead us voluntarily to cut back on our oh-so-enjoyable consumption of 'the necessities of life'?"

The secular viewpoint has no alternative but to appeal to self-interest, but self-interest is not sufficient motivation for people to live more simply, at least not over the long haul.

> Christians, however, don't have to be stuck in this boat. They have a rationale for the simple life that is infinitely superior to mere self-interest. And even more to the point, they have a gospel that goes far beyond man's saving himself by pulling at his own ecological bootstraps: it includes a God who can and will straighten out perversities and give men what it takes to discipline their rate of consumption, *first of all as a way of getting themselves correctly positioned to enjoy God,* and then—as an entirely free bonus—as an effective way of meeting the environmental crisis as well. And if this is the way it is with the Christian doctrine of the simple life, how tragic it would be if we were to trade it in for the ecological doctrine of sheer self-interest. (Eller, *The Simple Life,* p. 322, emphasis added)

For a Higher Cause

Jesus said that it would be hard for a person encumbered by wealth to enter the kingdom of God. He did not say it would be impossible, but he said it would be more difficult. He said those words to the sound of receding footsteps—a well-off young man whose "face fell" and who "went away sad" because Jesus had told him to sell what he had and give to the poor.

Immediately Peter put in a good word for the sacrifices he and his colleagues had made. "We have left everything to follow you!"

Jesus answered, "I tell you the truth, no one who has left home or brothers or sisters or mother or father or children or fields for me and the gospel will fail to receive a hundred times as much in this present age (homes, brothers, . . . —and with them, persecutions) and in the age to come, eternal life" (Mark 10:21-30).

The Christian's "giving up" is for the higher cause of the gospel. There are returns on what we give up for God—whether material goods or relationships. There will be food for us. There will be a place to live. There will be friends. There will be eternal life when the amount of those things enjoyed on earth no longer matters to us.

A sample system

We could be making more money in "real" jobs (that is, working full-time for somebody else) instead of being spottily self-employed. The work we are doing (at least at this time in our lives), combined with other involvements, gives us a sense of purpose. The level of income it produces has automatically simplified our lives and makes us consume less.

There is also another factor, freely chosen, that cuts down our consumption. It's a system of giving that has worked well for us for over twenty years. Here it is, put forth as an example, not as a directive. It's uncomplicated, direct, practical, and has tithing at its heart.

We are committed to giving, off the top, before taxes, before any other expenditures, a certain percentage of our income to the church and an equal percentage to missions. Since it's a habit of over twenty years, there's no agonizing over deciding how much to give away of every check; it's part of the budget, like the house payment and the utilities. It's already spent.

When a certain portion of income is voluntarily subtracted (and sent where it's needed) then our consumption is *automatically* cut back. If we don't have it, we can't spend it—assuming we don't go into debt. (We are also committed to avoiding debt—our home mortgage is the exception. You may say, "I have children in college, I can't live that way," but we aren't talking about what you have to do—we're talking about what we do.) Ronald J. Sider suggests a "graduated tithe" based on income: the higher the income, the higher the percentage of tithe.

Living this way automatically cuts down our consumption and use of resources not as an end in itself, but rather as a by-product of choosing to give. Our goal is not "cutting back" or "living simply," but "giving away."

Lots of times it looks like the tithe and mission offering is going to eat up the money for necessities, but the Lord has always faithfully provided housing, food, clothing, and transportation—not necessarily up to the standard of our neighbors, but so what? This is the way we live.

CHAPTER THIRTEEN

THE IDEALISM AND REALISM OF HOPE

I hope everything is as normal
as God has made it forever.
*letter in a Christmas card
from a Japanese teacher*

T*ap-tap-tap-tap-tap. Tap-tap-tap.* A gray squirrel sits on a
tree branch bared by winter. He's so busy gnawing on the
hard outer shell of a black walnut (the *tap-tap-tap* sound)
that he doesn't mind being closely watched by a human.

At first glance he looks "cute," a furry little guy sitting with a nut
in his front paws, busily nibbling away. A closer look reveals this is
life-and-death work. It's cold, food is scarce, and inside the walnut—
if he can get that shell off—is life-giving nourishment.

The squirrel is serious about his work. Serious—but not panicky.

Curiously enough it is nature itself that teaches us not to panic
about nature. The squirrel in the winter tree has a quality often seen
in wild animals, that sense of going about their business optimistical-
ly but in dead earnest. Not scared, not alarmed, just very busy doing
their jobs.

179

Creator and Sustainer

When Jesus told us to trust God for food and clothing—that is, to have faith that resources won't run out—he took his example from the flora and fauna of Palestine. "Look at the birds of the air; they do not sow or reap or store away in barns, and yet your heavenly Father feeds them." God "clothes" the plants of the field, he said, more splendidly than any king (Matt. 6:25-34).

Nature does not panic, because God the Creator is also God the Sustainer. Nature goes about its business neither in laziness nor in alarm, but in hope.

God is splendidly portrayed as both Creator and Sustainer in Psalm 104. The Lord "set the earth on its foundations; it can never be moved" (104:5). He made light, and clouds, and wind; he made the waters flow down and the land rise. God keeps life going by providing food and water for all living things on earth.

> These all look to you
>   to give them their food at the proper time.
> When you give it to them,
>   they gather it up;
> when you open your hand,
>   they are satisfied with good things.
> When you hide your face,
>   they are terrified;
> when you take away their breath,
>   they die and return to the dust.
> When you send your Spirit,
>   they are created,
>   and you renew the face of the earth. (Ps. 104:27-30)

Blue skies again?
The natural world lives in the peace of being cared for by the Creator and Sustainer. Humans, by contrast, are always worrying. A gloomy

mood pervades contemporary thinking, whether about the economy or the environment. Hope is in short supply.

Just now I looked out the window and gasped. The sky is a delicate blue streaked with white. I wondered why it looked so surprising till I realized that for many days the sky has been overcast with not a bit of blue showing through.

In his book *What Went Wrong?* the Englishman Jeremy Seabrook writes about the dissatisfaction of the British laboring person. For years the English working class struggled for better working conditions and better wages, but now that they have achieved both, the spoils of victory are not what was expected. "Despite spectacular material improvements," Seabrook says, "there persists in working-class communities a malaise, an anger, a bitterness." Progress has come at the expense of human relationships.

> If you talk to old working-class people, however oppressive the poverty and insecurity under which they lived, they will always recall that the greatest consolation was the quality of the human relationships; how comforting it was to share, with kin, neighbours, work companions. But now, in the face of the vast improvements in material conditions, it is the people who are all wrong. Things are better; but all that has been gained has been at the expense of human relationships. (Seabrook, *What Went Wrong?* p. 13)

That was England in the late 1970s. Are things any better now in America?

"Down in the Dumps" is what a recent *Newsweek* calls us and asks, "If the numbers aren't so bad, why is the country feeling so lousy?" True, there are layoffs, evictions, and lost home equity.

> It's only logical for people to feel bad. On the other hand, it's crazy. This is occurring at the precise moment that America's great historic rival has literally disappeared from the map, taking with it the threat of nuclear holocaust that loomed so large in the

boom years of the mid-'80s. On the evidence, it would seem that "consumer confidence" bears an inverse relationship to the prospect of human survival, which is ridiculous even by the standard of economics. (Adler, "Down in the Dumps," *Newsweek)*

In the piles of environmental writings we've read while working on this book, there is the same sense of gloom and doom. The earth is in peril, and things are going from bad to worse.

Is there any "blue sky" for life on earth? Is there any hope that shows through despite all the gloom and doom? Specifically, do Christians have any hope?

All burned up anyway?

"Ecology? Why bother? It's all going to get burned up anyway."

So said a man at a sustainable-farming gathering. In the here and now, he sold shares in a large communal garden but obviously was not looking for this world to be "sustainable" forever.

He seems to have Scripture on his side. For centuries Christians have taken comfort in 2 Peter 3 when people scoff, "Where is the promise of his coming?" The return of Christ is "slow" only to our finite minds, Peter says, because to the Lord a day is like a thousand years, and a thousand years is like a day.

> But the day of the Lord will come as a thief in the night; in the which the heavens shall pass away with a great noise, and the elements shall melt with fervent heat, the earth also and the works that are therein shall be burned up.
>
> Seeing then that all these things shall be dissolved, what manner of persons ought ye to be in all holy conversation and godliness,
>
> Looking for and hasting unto the coming of the day of God, wherein the heavens being on fire shall be dissolved, and the elements shall melt with fervent heat?
>
> Nevertheless we, according to his promise, look for new

heavens and a new earth, wherein dwelleth righteousness. (2 Pet. 3:10-13, KJV)

The promise rings with drama even as it comforts. It seems to say that when Christ returns, all this physical world that we have loved or resisted or tamed or damaged will be destroyed, and God will then start over with "new heavens and a new earth."

It's hard for us to imagine "new heavens," but we would certainly be delighted in a "new earth" made exactly as God wants—pure, undamaged by sin. Then everything would at last be in harmony, and the ecology would be just as God planned it.

It is a biblical truth that our personal future does not depend on this physical world being saved. We are secure in God no matter what happens to this planet. Though some will immediately call that "pie in the sky" and an avoidance of responsibility to this earth, it is still absolutely true that the Christian's ultimate hope is not in this physical world. *Even if* it freezes or blows up, we are secure in Christ, because "whether we live or die, we belong to the Lord" (Rom. 14:8).

A Disappointing Prophecy?

Still many Christians would admit that (though they believe the Bible wholeheartedly) they cringe a little at the idea of the earth being burned up.

First of all, doesn't it make Christian environmentalism an exercise in futility? After we have poured so much energy and effort and emotion into healing and restoring this earth, in obedience to God, is he going to turn around and destroy it?

Second, and more urgent, doesn't it give everyone a terrible license to use and abuse this earth with no regard for its future? If it's all going to get burned up anyway, why try to save it?

We can give an immediate answer to both those objections by saying that God *calls us to obey* him regardless of consequences, and *to be good stewards* of his creation here and now regardless of what will happen to it later.

After all, most of the things we daily handle with care are temporary. We cook meals that give nutrition for only a few hours. We teach Sunday school lessons that are often forgotten by Monday. We witness to some people who will never accept Christ. We build houses, we paint them, landscape them, and decorate them, and they will eventually fall down. Yet God calls us to do all these things faithfully, even if they appear to have no eternal results.

In his book *Against the Night,* Charles Colson challenges Christians to offer a living alternative to the ideas shaping our society. Then he asks a pointed question:

> Will we succeed?
> Perhaps.
> Does it matter? In one sense, yes, of course. In another sense, not really. For our duty is clear no matter what the outcome. (Colson, *Against the Night,* p. 182)

The same can be said of Christian efforts in ecology. Our duty to God's creation, over which we are given dominion, is "clear no matter what the outcome."

On the other hand, there may be another side to the certainty that the earth will be "burned up."

Burning or purifying?

During the research for this book, someone suggested that 2 Peter 3:10 could also be interpreted to mean that the earth will be "purified." It was an intriguing idea, but it sounded a bit like interpreting Scripture to fit a particular need. On the other hand, the Bible and church history are filled with so many misinterpretations of "prediction" prophecies with only a few correct ones (such as Daniel 9:2 and Matthew 2:4-5), that we felt we couldn't say all the evidence was in for the meaning of 2 Peter 3:10. At any rate this idea of "purification" seemed worth exploring.

We cannot speak authoritatively on either Greek or the "end of the world," but there is some evidence that the burning on the day of Christ will be one of purifying rather than destruction.

Evidence of ancient manuscripts

If you read the *New International Version,* you've noticed that 2 Peter 3:10 does not say, "The earth and everything in it will be *burned up*" but rather, "The earth and everything in it will be *laid bare.*" These days there are so many modern English translations of the Bible that our ears are accustomed to hearing alternative versions of Scripture. But *laid bare* as a synonym for *burned up*? How could the translators have come up with such different interpretations?

The answer is: they didn't.

The books of the New Testament are the best-attested of all ancient books. We have more than 5,000 Greek manuscripts or pieces of manuscripts that are ancient copies of New Testament books, and the discovery process is still going on. From these copies we have solid ground on which to try to reconstruct the originals. That is how Bible translators work. By comparing the oldest and most reliable manuscripts, they try to determine as accurately as possible the text of the original writing.

As with all the New Testament books, the many copies of 2 Peter agree in remarkable detail. We do *not* have twenty wildly divergent versions of 2 Peter floating around. But occasionally the manuscripts differ on a word or a phrase. The variations in 2 Peter 3:10 come from such "variant readings" in the ancient texts.

The earliest manuscripts have the word *heurethesetai,* "will be laid bare" or "will be discovered," with the root from which we get "eureka." That is the word chosen by the translators of the *New International Version* and the *New English Bible.* Other ancient manuscripts have *katakaesetai,* "will be burned up"; you'll find that

in the *Revised Standard Version* and the *New American Standard.*
There are some other variants, including the word for "disappear,"
preferred by *Today's English Version* and *J.B. Phillips.*

There is no deception going on here. In most Bibles there is a
footnote at 2 Peter 3:10 explaining that other readings are possible.

Testing our work

What would be the point of things on earth being "discovered" or
"laid bare" at Christ's coming?

One of Paul's letters has a fascinating parallel. Paul wrote that
when Christ returns, the work of each of us will be "shown for what
it is, because the Day will bring it to light." How will it be revealed?
By fire, "and the fire will test the quality of each man's work." Gold,
silver, and costly stones will endure; wood, hay, and straw will be
burned up. Figuratively speaking, useless works will be destroyed
and good works will be purified (1 Cor. 3:10-15).

Even if the correct word at the end of 2 Peter 3:10 is the one for
"burned up," it's intriguing that it's the same word used in the
Gospels for the burning of *chaff* and *weeds* while the grain is spared
(Matt. 3:12; 13:30, 40; Luke 3:17)—another image of purifying the
good by getting rid of the bad.

Then what about the phrase "will be destroyed by fire" (NIV) or
"shall melt with fervent heat" (KJV) in verse 10? And what about the
restatement of the fiery destruction in verse 12?

"Destroy" or "melt" in verse 10 are translations of the very common Greek word *luo,* "to loose," "to dissolve," "to untie." The word
also appears in verses 11 and 12. The "fire" or "fervent heat" is the
root of our word *cauterize;* it was used as a medical term, of a fever,
and it re-appears in verse 12. "Being on fire" or "by fire" in verse 12
is from the root *pur* and is related to refining of gold by fire in 1 Peter
1:7 and Revelation 3:18 (Metzger, *A Textual Commentary on The
Greek New Testament,* pp. 705-706; Brown, *The Jerome Bible Com-*

mentary, p. 498; Blum, *The Expositor's Bible Commentary,* p. 286; Vine, *An Expository Dictionary of New Testament Words).*

A good earth

The idea of the earth being burned up because it is evil is much more of a Greek gnostic idea than a Hebrew idea. Though the New Testament often speaks negatively about "the world," the word used is *kosmos* or "world system." The word "earth," *gee,* is always used in a positive sense. When Jesus spoke of heaven and earth *(gee)* disappearing, it was to illustrate the contrasting eternal dependability of his words (Matt. 5:18; 24:35).

Could it be that this coming fire is purifying rather than destroying? Which interpretation is more consistent with the rest of Scripture? The earth being purified seems more consistent with the statement that the earth "can never be moved" (Ps. 104:5). It is also more consistent with Romans 8:19-21 (emphasis added):

> The creation *waits in eager expectation* for the sons of God to be revealed. For the creation was subjected to frustration, not by its own choice, but by the will of the one who subjected it, in hope that the creation itself will be *liberated from its bondage to decay and brought into the glorious freedom* of the children of God.

The creation that exists now can hardly be said to have "hope" if it is only going to be destroyed. It will hardly be "liberated" and "brought into glorious freedom" if it is going to be annihilated. Hope and liberation would be more appropriate to earth if it were going to be renewed, restored, and remade.

We are playing with ideas, but the ideas are about real things. We are speculating, but it is a real event about which we speculate. *Something* will happen to this present creation when Christ returns, and whatever it is, it will be good for the world and for "all who have longed for his appearing" (2 Tim. 4:8).

Meanwhile . . .

Whatever God's plans for the earth, we live here now. "The Son of Man will come at an hour when you do not expect him" (Matt. 24:44), but in the meantime we have our jobs to do on earth.

The last thing God's care for the earth gives us is a license to quit doing our God-given jobs. If we want food and clothing, we are still expected to sow and reap, spin and sew. Likewise if we want to preserve and heal the earth, we have work to do. But in all our work we must remain conscious that "apart from me you can do nothing" (John 15:5b).

We are the Lord's ambassadors, representing him on earth, but the work is not entirely up to us. The ambassador represents the home government but is not responsible for carrying out all of the activity of the government. Christians' work for the environment can be free of the frantic tone (even panic) that accompanies some environmental efforts. What egoists we would be if we thought that the God who created the world had left its rescue entirely up to us. At the same time, the fact that God cares for the earth does not mean we can stop caring for it.

Creation waits, and we wait for the coming of Christ—but we "wait" like the servant in Jesus' parable in Matthew 24:45-51 and Luke 12:42-46. His master put him in charge of the household and then went out of sight, leaving the servant in a nice house with plenty to do and plenty of temptations not to do it and to take advantage of his position.

"Who then is the faithful and wise servant, whom the master has put in charge of the servants in his household to give them their food at the proper time? It will be good for that servant whose master finds him *doing so* when he returns" (Matt. 24:45-46). But if he "begins to beat his fellow servants and to eat and drink with drunkards"—to mistreat the other people in the house and to use up the master's resources for his own pleasure—then he is in trouble (Matt. 24:49).

Without a clear and universal awakening to the fact that humanity's role in nature is that of a steward responsible to fulfilling a prior covenant between God and the entire created order (Gen. 9:12-13), and that *if man refuses to fulfill that role he is in mortal danger of forfeiting his reason for being,* any humanistic or sentimental appeal to man's obligations to the natural environment will be fruitless. . . . Why should anyone care anything about nature except in exploitable possibilities, if there is no universally recognized essential connection between humanity and nature? (Rossi, "The Eleventh Commandment: Toward an Ethic of Ecology," *Epiphany Journal,* emphasis added)

The best-kept secret in environmental writing is that Christians (so often blamed for ecological damage) are doing much more for ecology than the world would like to admit.

Sometimes they are missionaries like Doug Johnson of the Covenant Church in Thailand.

Pigs, ducks, and fish

Doug Johnson, Covenant Church missionary to Thailand, tells us of sustainable cooperative farming going on there.

Over 90 percent of the people of northeast Thailand are poor rice farmers. In the fall, after rice harvest, 60 percent must leave to go find work in the city. The yearly exodus disrupts both family life and the hope of building a strong Thai church in the rural areas.

Thai Christians are using their available resources (pigs, ducks, small ponds, grass, and fish) in a series of "integrated ecosystem cooperatives." The farm system works like this:

There is a fish pond next to a pig pen. A rice mill provides cracked rice and bran for feed for the pigs and for ducks that also swim in the pond. Waste from the pigs and ducks, along with grass, is put into the pond in compost mounds—excellent fertilizer for plankton and other plants that thrive in the sunny pond. Five kinds of fish eat at different levels in the pond, not competing with each other for food. Grass growing at the pond's edge controls erosion and provides food for carp. Dead fish are put into another pond for catfish. The fish thrive and grow large, then they are harvested and sold.

The aim is to use everything on the cooperative farm and waste as little as possible. The Covenant mission does not own the farmland; the land is owned by a Thai foundation.

The farms produce a stable income so the farmers don't have to leave their villages each year. They are a resource for spiritual growth as they encourage responsibility, service, and cooperation. They provide good food to keep the people healthy; a church burdened by disease has little energy for ministry (Doug Johnson, program and interview).

Sometimes the Christians who make a difference are not missionaries officially sanctioned by a mission organization. Often they are just Christians who have decided to care. They have weighed their values and decided that a life of following God into the midst of earth's problems is better than a life of ephemeral "security."

Hope's seventeen acres

Deo and Elaine Miller, highly successful Southern California contractors, went to Sri Lanka on a "tropical paradise vacation." God surprised them. They found their hearts broken in "Hell's Seventeen Acres," where thousands of squatter families lived in poverty and despair on the outskirts of the city of Colombo in what Art Beals called a "human dumping ground."

[Deo and Elaine] exchanged a prosperous business and a comfortable Southern California hillside ranch house, complete with garden and swimming pool, for a cramped, hot flat in a Colombo apartment building. They spent their days developing cottage industries, vocational training opportunities, and feeding centers for the malnourished children. . . . They knew . . . it wasn't going to be quick. It wasn't going to generate "positive press reports" in the churches back home. . . . It may still be "Hell's Seventeen

Acres" . . . but a new resident is becoming known in the shanties, streets, and alleyways. A new face. A new force. Its name is Hope. (Beals, *Beyond Hunger,* pp. 178-179)

Beginning

Suppose you want to be involved in making a difference and bringing hope to earth. Where do you start?

First, examine your values. As Christians, we don't need to accept all of the blame for the environmental crisis, but we do share some of the blame. We need to examine our lives as individuals and as church communities to see how we have merely absorbed society's values that are detrimental to ecology. We need to establish new values based on our worship and trust in a loving God: a worship and trust that care for his creation and its people.

In your use of resources, consumption of goods, and finances, are you living in a way that "serves" the natural world and other people and "guards" them—seeks to protect and nourish rather than to destroy? Big plans for helping the earth "sometime" or "elsewhere" are pointless if we aren't living consistently in the little things here and now.

Next, take stock of your gifts. What do you have to offer? You may not have the financial resources of Deo and Elaine Miller, but you have abilities that God can use.

Hard as it is, take a look at your work. Does it "serve" and "guard" creation? Does it seek to protect and nourish people and the natural world rather than to use and destroy them? Does it bring the satisfaction and meaning to your life that you desire?

Mission agencies often have need for people with skills of agricultural development, health care, teaching, or cottage-industry development, to name a few areas. You may not have to change careers to take advantage of the openings. There are opportunities for short-term volunteer workers both with mission agencies and relief agencies. Short-term volunteers often don't need to get specific technical training in advance since they will be working alongside trained workers. Incidentally, in your giving to mission and relief organizations, inquire about their efforts toward ecologically sound development—for example, sustainable agriculture. Encourage and support those efforts.

Most exciting, you do not have to be locked into the channels and opportunities presented by somebody else. Use your imagination to think about how *your* skills can help the world be cleaner, can promote respect for life, can help other people become self-sufficient.

Opportunities unlimited
Most of us are afraid we're going to have to choose between a better environment and a satisfying standard of living. The good news is that we can have both, though that doesn't necessarily mean we can maintain our present way of life along with sound ecology. It does mean we can have more satisfying lives even while we "wait" along with earth for the promised renewal. The opportunities for making more money and greater security may be becoming more scarce, but opportunities to worship God and care for his creation are unlimited.

BIBLIOGRAPHY

Adler, Jerry. "Down in the Dumps." *Newsweek,* January 13, 1992, pp. 18-19.

Ahlstrom, Sydney E. *A Religious History of the American People.* New Haven, Conn.: Yale University Press, 1972.

Alexander, Brooks. "Tragedy & Hope in Genesis 3." *Spiritual Counterfeits Project Journal,* 8:1 (1988), p. 29.

Anderson, B.W. "Creation." *The Interpreter's Dictionary of the Bible,* Vol. 1, p. 729. Nashville: Abingdon Press, 1962.

Ann Landers column. Ashland, Wisconsin *Daily Press,* September 26, 1991, p. 16.

Bacon, Francis. *Novum Organum,* in *The English Philosophers from Bacon to Mill.* Edwin A. Burtt, ed. New York: Random House, 1939.

Barry, Dave. "Notes on Western Civilization." *Chicago Tribune Magazine,* July 28, 1991, quoted in *Christianity Today,* December 16, 1991, p. 48.

Beals, Art, and Larry Libby. *Beyond Hunger.* Portland, Oreg.: Multnomah Press, 1985.

Beisner, E. Calvin. *Prospects for Growth: A Biblical View of Population, Resources, and the Future.* Wheaton, Ill.: Crossway Books, 1990.

Bentham, Jeremy. *An Introduction to the Principles of Morals and Legislation,* quoted in Roderick Frazier Nash, *The Rights of Nature: A History of Environmental Ethics,* Madison, Wis.: University of Wisconsin Press, 1989.

Blackman, Ann, Tom Curry, and Edwin M. Reingold. "Crybabies: Eternal Victims." *Time,* August 12, 1991, p. 17.

Blum, Edwin A., ed. *The Expositor's Bible Commentary.* Grand Rapids, Mich.: Zondervan, 1981.

Brost, Mike, in *Northern View.* Ashland, Wisconsin *Daily Press,* Sept. 20, 1991, p. 5.

Brown, Raymond E., ed. *The Jerome Bible Commentary.* Englewood Cliffs, N.J.: Prentice-Hall, 1968.

Bullock, Wilbur L. "The Coming Catastrophes: Causes and Remedies." *Journal of the American Scientific Association,* September 1969, p. 85.

Castro, Janice. "The Simple Life." *Time,* April 8, 1991, p. 58.

Cerio, Gregory. "The Black Legend: Were the Spaniards *That* Cruel?" *Newsweek* Special Edition on Columbus, Fall/Winter 1991, p. 51.

Chevre, Stuart. "The Gaia Hypothesis: Science, Mythology, and the Desecration of God." *SCP Journal,* 16:1 (1991), p. 30.

Colson, Charles. *Against the Night.* Ann Arbor, Mich.: Servant Publications, 1989.

Commager, Henry Steele. *The Empire of Reason.* Garden City, N.Y.: Anchor Press/Doubleday, 1977.

Commoner, Barry. *Making Peace with the Planet.* New York: Pantheon Books, 1990.

Cooper, Tim. *Green Christianity.* London: Hodder & Stoughton, 1990.

Daggett, Dan. "Western Range Reels Under Cattle Onslaught." *Audubon Activist,* September 1991, p. 1.

Daly, Herman E., and John B. Cobb, Jr. *For the Common Good.* Boston: Beacon Press, 1989.

Devall, Bill, and George Sessions. *Deep Ecology: Living As If Nature Mattered.* Layton, Utah: Gibbs M. Smith, Inc., 1985.

DeWitt, Calvin B. "The Religious Foundations of Ecology." *The Mother Earth Handbook,* edited by Judith S. Scherff, p. 253. New York: Continuum, 1991.

Dillard, Annie. *Pilgrim at Tinker Creek.* New York: Harper's Magazine Press, 1974. Harper & Row edition 1990.

Dubos, Rene. *The Wooing of Earth.* New York: Charles Scribner's Sons, 1980.

Dyrness, William A. "Are We Our Planet's Keeper?" *Christianity Today,* April 8, 1991, p. 41.

Eastep, Wayne. "Nomads of the Desert." *Smithsonian,* December 1984, pp. 46-56.

Easterbrook, Gregg. "Cleaning Up." *Newsweek,* July 24, 1989, pp. 29, 41.

Ehrlich, Anne H., and Paul R. Ehrlich. *Earth.* New York: Franklin Watts, 1987.

Eller, Vernard. *The Simple Life: The Christian Stance Toward Possessions.* Grand Rapids, Mich.: Eerdmans, 1973.

Ellul, Jacques. *The Technological Society,* tr. John Wilkinson. N.Y.: Alfred A. Knopf, Inc., 1964.

Elmer-DeWitt, Philip. "Gee, Your Car Smells Terrific!" *Time,* July 22, 1991, p. 48.

Farrant, Sally. "Enduring Hunger." *Tear Times,* Autumn 1991, p. 8.

"The Fight for Land Rights." *Tear Times,* Autumn 1990, p. 6.

Fox, Matthew. *The Coming of the Cosmic Christ.* San Francisco: Harper & Row, 1988.

Freudenberger, C. Dean. *Global Dust Bowl.* Minneapolis: Augsburg, 1990.

Garrett, Samuel. "Jonathan Edwards and the Great Awakening." *American Christianity: A Case Approach.* Ronald C. White, Jr., Louis B. Weeks, and Garth M. Rosell, eds., Grand Rapids, Mich.: Eerdmans, 1986.

Gaustad, Edward Scott. *A Religious History of America.* New York: Harper & Row, 1966.

Gay, Peter. *Age of Enlightenment.* New York: Time Inc., 1966.

Gilbert, Douglas, and Clyde S. Kilby. *C.S. Lewis: Images of His World.* Grand Rapids, Mich.: Eerdmans, 1973.

Goldsmith, Edward and Nicholas Hildyard, eds. *The Earth Report.* Los Angeles: Price Stern Sloan, Inc., 1988.

Goudzwaard, Bob. *Capitalism and Progress.* Grand Rapids, Mich: Eerdmans, 1979.

_____. *Idols of Our Time.* Downers Grove, Ill.: Inter-Varsity Press, 1984.

Granberg-Michaelson, Wesley. "At the Dawn of the New Creation." *Sojourners, November 1981.*

_____. *A Worldly Spirituality.* San Francisco: Harper & Row, 1984.

Gruchow, Paul. *The Necessity of Empty Places.* New York: St. Martin's Press, 1988.

Hale, John R. *Renaissance.* New York: Time Inc., 1965.

Houston, James. "Faith on the Line." Interview in *SCP Journal,* 8:1 (1988), p. 15.

Johnson, Doug. Program and interview, May 12, 1991.

Kavanaugh, John Francis. *Following Christ in a Consumer Society.* Maryknoll, New York: Orbis Books, 1981.

Keen, Sam. "Original Blessing, Not Original Sin." *Psychology Today,* June 1989, pp. 56-57.

Kyser, Leila L. "A Logger's Lament." *Newsweek,* October 22, 1990, p. 10.

Lappe, Frances Moore, and Joseph Collins. *World Hunger: Ten Myths.* San Francisco: Institute for Food and Development Policy, 1977.

Lawrence, D.H. "The Rocking-Horse Winner." In *The Oxford Book of Short Stories,* pp. 273-289. New York: Oxford University Press, 1981.

Leake, Andrew. "The Fight for Land Rights." *Tear Times,* Autumn 1990, p. 6.

Leopold, Aldo. *A Sand County Almanac.* New York: Oxford University Press, 1949.

Levinson, Marc. "Living on the Edge." *Newsweek,* November 4, 1991, pp. 23-25.

Lewis, C.S. *The Abolition of Man.* The Macmillan Co., 1947.

Lewis, Sinclair. *Babbitt,* New American Library edition. New York: Harcourt, Brace & World, Inc., 1922.

"Life and Death of the Rainforest." *Tear Times,* Autumn 1990, p. 9.

Lovelock, J.E. *The Ages of Gaia: A Biography of Our Living Earth.* N.Y.: W.W. Norton & Co., 1988.

_____. *Gaia: A New Look at Life on Earth.* Oxford, England: Oxford University Press, 1979.

McDonagh, Sean. *To Care for the Earth: A Call to a New Theology.* Santa Fe: Bear & Co., 1986.

McKibben, Bill. *The End of Nature.* New York: Random House, 1989.

Metzger, Bruce M., ed. *A Textual Commentary on the Greek New Testament.* N.Y.: United Bible Societies, 1975.

Mill, John Stuart. *Principles of Political Economy.* New York: Longmans, Green, and Co., 1909.

Miller, Perry. *The American Puritans.* Garden City, N.Y.: Doubleday, 1956.

Moncrief, Lewis. "The Cultural Basis for Our Environmental Crisis." *Science,* October 1970, pp. 58-59, 63.

"Moon Dust for Sale." Ashland, Wisconsin *Daily Press,* January 6, 1992, p. 4.

Morrow, Lance. "A Nation of Finger Pointers." *Time,* August 12, 1991, p. 15.

Nash, Roderick Frazier. *The Rights of Nature: A History of Environmental Ethics.* Madison, Wis.: University of Wisconsin Press, 1989.

Olson, Sigurd. *Of Time and Place.* New York: Alfred A. Knopf, 1982.

Passmore, John. *Man's Responsibility for Nature.* New York: Charles Scribner's Sons, 1974.

Peterson, Eugene H. *Earth & Altar.* Downers Grove, Ill.: InterVarsity Press, 1985.

Rabe, Ken. "A Day in Earth Court." *GreenNet,* November-December 1990/January 1991, p. 7.

Rand, Stephen. "A Harvest for Africa." *Tear Times,* Autumn 1991, pp. 5-6.

Rauschenbusch, Walter. *Christianity and the Social Crisis.* New York: Macmillian Co., 1907.

Restoring Creation for Ecology and Justice. Louisville, Ky.: Office of the General Assembly, Presbyterian Church (USA), 1990.

Richards, Caroline. "The Nature-Culture Dilemma." *Breakthrough.* Winter/Summer 1990, p. 8.

Rifkin, Jeremy, with Ted Howard. *The Emerging Order: God in the Age of Scarcity.* New York: G.P. Putnam's Sons, 1979.

Rolston, Holmes, III. *Philosophy Gone Wild.* Buffalo, N.Y.: Prometheus Books, 1986.

Rossi, Fr. Vincent. "The Eleventh Commandment: Toward an Ethic of Ecology." *Epiphany Journal,* Summer 1981, p. 8.

_____. "Theocentrism: The Cornerstone of Christian Ecology." *Epiphany Journal,* Fall 1985, p. 8, 15.

Satchell, Michael. "A Vicious 'Circle of Poison.'" *U.S. News & World Report,* June 10, 1991, pp. 31-32.

Schaeffer, Francis A. *Escape from Reason.* Downers Grove, Ill.: InterVarsity Press, 1968.

_____. *How Should We Then Live?* Old Tappan, N.J.: Fleming H. Revell, 1976.

_____ . *Pollution and the Death of Man.* Wheaton, Ill.: Tyndale House, 1970.

Seabrook, Jeremy. *What Went Wrong?* New York: Pantheon Books, 1978.

Sesame Street Magazine. November 1991, p. 11.

Shapiro, Walter. "The Birth and—Maybe—Death of Yuppiedom." *Time,* April 8, 1991, p. 65.

Sheldon, Joseph K., chart: "Twenty-One Years after 'The Historical Roots of our Ecologic Crisis': How Has the Church Responded?"

Shi, David E. *In Search of the Simple Life.* Salt Lake City: Peregrine Smith, 1986.

Sider, Ronald J. "Green Theology." *ESA Advocate,* July/August 1991, pp. 1, 3.

Simon, Edith. *The Reformation.* New York: Time Inc., 1966.

Sittler, Joseph Jr. "A Theology for Earth." *The Christian Scholar,* September 1954, p. 370.

Stager, Lawrence E. "The Song of Deborah." *Biblical Archaeology Review,* January/February 1989, p. 55.

Steffen, Lloyd. "In Defense of Dominion." unpublished paper, p. 1.

Steinbeck, John. *Travels with Charley.* New York: Viking Press, 1961.

Theroux, Paul. "Malawi: Faces of A Quiet Land." *National Geographic,* September 1989, p. 386.

Touching. Wheaton, Ill.: World Relief. Fall 1990, pp. 2-3.

Trefil, James. "Modeling Earth's Future Climate Requires Both Science and Guesswork." *Smithsonian,* December 1990, pp. 29-37.

Tuan, Yi-Fu. "Our Treatment of the Environment in Ideal and Actuality." *American Scientist,* 58:248 (1970).

Turner, John W. "Given a Free Rein, Prolific Mustangs Gallop into Trouble." *Smithsonian,* February 1984, pp. 88-96.

Turque, Bill. "The War for the West." *Newsweek,* September 30, 1991, pp. 23-25.

Verne, Jules. *Twenty Thousand Leagues Under the Sea.* New York: Charles Scribner's Sons, 1925.

Vine, W.E., *An Expository Dictionary of New Testament Words.* London: Oliphants Ltd., 1940.

Webb, Mike. "Death of the Rainforest." *Tear Times,* Autumn 1990, pp. 3-5.

White, Lynn, Jr. "The Historical Roots of Our Ecologic Crisis." *Science,* March 10, 1967, pp. 1203-1207.

Wilkinson, Loren. "Cosmic Christology and the Christian's Role in Creation." *Christian Scholar's Review,* 11:1 (1981), p. 21.

Williams, Lindsey. *The Energy Non-Crisis.* Wheatridge, Colo.: Worth Publishing Co., 1980.

Wood, Arthur. "The Intimacy of Jesus with Nature." *London Quarterly & Holborn Review,* 189:45 (1964).

Wright, Richard T. *Biology Through the Eyes of Faith.* San Francisco: Harper & Row, 1989.